BASIC
BUDGETING
PRACTICES
for Librarians

BASIC BUDGETING PRACTICES
for Librarians

Margo C. Trumpeter

Richard S. Rounds

CHICAGO
American Library Association
1985

Designed by Charles Bozett

Composed by Impressions, Inc.
in Baskerville and Optima on a
Penta-driven Autologic APS μ5
phototypesetting system

Printed on 50-pound Glatfelter,
a pH-neutral stock, and bound
in B-grade Holliston Roxite linen
cloth by Braun-Brumfield, Inc.

Library of Congress Cataloging in Publication Data

Trumpeter, Margo C.
  Basic budgeting practices for librarians.

  Includes index.
  1. Library finance. 2. Program budgeting. 3. Budget.
I. Rounds, Richard S. II. Title
Z683.T78   1985   025.1'1   84-20503
ISBN   0-8389-0399-1

Contents

Figures

Preface

What do you do as library administrator? You plan, organize, and control responsibilities that cannot be performed well without a budget.[1]

As a management tool, your budget becomes your plan for future activities. Without this plan, you could not organize, staff, develop, or coordinate the library's activities knowledgeably. Without this plan, you would have no standards or expectations against which to evaluate the library's programs. It follows, therefore, that the skills of budgeting, both technical and political, are at the heart of good administration.

You can learn these skills on the firing line or you can study them before you practice them. You can be taught by a professor in class, or by your library director, or you can teach yourself. This text is designed to help you teach yourself, and for use by students, aspiring administrators, and practicing administrators of public and school libraries. Where appropriate, two sets of practice experiences accommodate those who are library administrators and those who are not.

1. P. A. Thomas and Valerie A. Ward, *An Analysis of Managerial Activities in Libraries*, Aslib Occupational Publication No. 14 (London: Aslib, 1974), p. 3.

1
What Services Are Provided to Whom?

Why Does Your Library Exist?

All libraries are committed to meeting information needs of their communities and all public libraries share a common mission of meeting their cultural, educational, and recreational needs as well.[1] But the needs of each community differ so that the role of each library will emphasize different services to different clientele.

To help identify your library's role, you will need to gather some basic data into three informational packages:

> A community profile
> An evaluation of the library's current services
> Measures of the performance of the library

This chapter presents a general overview of the process developed by Palmour, Bellassai, and DeWath at the direction of the Public Library Association of the American Library Association. Their study, *A Planning Process for Public Libraries*, published by ALA in 1980, is recommended as a necessary supplement to this chapter.

Program budget formats require identification of existing services and establishment of priorities and alternatives. Although line-item budget formats often allow the use of money to continue unchallenged from year to year, funds are now scarce and the competition among public agencies is keen. As a result, even if you are using a

---

1. Public Library Association Goals, Guideline, and Standards Committee, *The Public Library Mission Statement and Its Imperatives for Service* (Chicago: ALA, 1979).

line-item budget, you must occasionally reassess your community and the library's role in it. By using a systematic planning process, you will gather data you can use in setting priorities, assigning costs, and pursuing funding.

Community Profile

A community profile summarizes the population, industries, and services available in a community. This information can be found in secondary sources, especially census data, but also reports prepared by the Chamber of Commerce, local planning documents, and the advertising departments of local newspapers, etc.

CENSUS DATA

Imagine the case of a branch librarian, noted for her excellent children's program, who noticed a sharp decline in program attendance. The director was sure the librarian had "lost her touch." She, on the other hand, blamed the intolerance of some of her elderly patrons for frightening the children away. After examining trends in the ages of neighborhood residents and household sizes through census data,[2] they both realized that the predominance of households had changed to single-member households and the elderly population had increased considerably. Young families were moving into the northern side of the city, where low-cost housing was going up. Once the library director understood the facts, it was easy to make staffing and programming decisions for both the South and North branches of the library.

The census data most useful to library managers are census tracts. Having a population averaging 4,000, census tracts are fairly homogeneous with respect to population characteristics, economic status, and living conditions. Your state library can provide you with maps of the census tracts in your service area. Using the data for the tracts served by your library, you can easily determine race, gender, educational and income levels, occupations, and household sizes for each area you serve. Figure 1 provides a way to organize the census information that will be most useful to you.

2. U.S. Department of Commerce, Bureau of the Census, *General Population Characteristics, 1980 Census of Population.*

	Census Tract			Community	
	1960	1970	1980	1980	Census Tract as Percent of Community
Total population	____	____	____	____	____
Percent of population change each decade	____	____	____	____	____
Percent of population age 25+	____	____	____	____	____
Median age of population	____	____	____	____	____
Percent of population over 25 with less than 12 years school completed	____	____	____	____	____
With high school graduation	____	____	____	____	____
13+ years of school completed	____	____	____	____	____
Median years school completed	____	____	____	____	____
Median family income	____	____	____	____	____

Figure 1. Organizing Census Information

OTHER INFORMATION

Population characteristics are not the only data to consider. Information on business and industry can be crucial, too.[3] For example, a director of a library was puzzled by the heavy circulation of romances when census data showed a concentration of highly educated professionals in the area served. After securing business and industry information, he realized that hundreds of the expected library users were commuting to work outside the community. The library was serving the information needs of the remaining, less highly educated, blue-collar population. Now the director realized why romances were popular, and changed library emphases to meet the information needs of this public.

3. U.S. Department of Commerce, Bureau of the Census, *County Business Patterns.*

Along with population characteristics and data about business and industry, the community profile should reveal the existence of social clubs, recreational facilities, cultural activities, community and special-interest groups. If your city lacks organized activities, you may want to pursue special programs and promote use of the library's meeting rooms. But if there are numerous clubs and groups, your efforts to provide programs which may duplicate what is already available will be unnecessary. Take note of educational facilities, museums, and other types of libraries. By assessing your relationship with those other information resources, you may gain insights into possibilities of resource sharing and nonduplication of efforts.

Library Services

A community profile will give you general background to help determine the library's potential role in the community. Some data will not be useful to you as a decision maker until they can be paired with information on current library services.

You are probably already collecting statistics on current library services. To be meaningful, they should be prepared annually and then cumulated to reveal year-to-year trends over a five-year period. Data should be collected on each item listed below and prepared in a format like that suggested in figure 2.

SOURCES OF INCOME

Why do you care about the sources of income as long as you are getting the money? A chart helps you compare the percentage of funds from different sources over a five-year period. Each year, calculate the part of the total coming from local, state, and federal sources, gifts, and miscellaneous revenues. You will be able to note any significant increases or decreases in support from source to source. The finance committee may then be instructed that federal or state revenues are steadily decreasing, so that they are obliged to appropriate enough money locally to maintain levels of service.

PER CAPITA INCOME

Your total budget becomes more meaningful when you compute it on a per capita basis and calculate its purchasing power. These figures can be charted to show increases and decreases over a five-year period.

Per capita income is computed by dividing the library's total income by the total population:

$$\$380,000 \;/\; 50,000 = \$7.60$$

If last year's per capita income had been $7.40, the increase was 3 percent:

$$\$7.60 \;/\; \$7.40 = 1.027$$

$$1.027 - 1 = .027, \text{ roughly } 3\%$$

Any increase in per capita support means little until you discover whether that increase will provide more purchasing power than last year's budget, taking inflation into account. Assuming you are budgeting with a July to June fiscal year, you can use the CPI (Consumer Price Index) for the midpoint of each year.[4] For example, the CPI in mid-1982 was 282.5, and in the midpoint of 1981 it had been 260.5. To calculate the rate of inflation from one year to the next, subtract the current year's CPI from that of the previous year; then divide the difference by the CPI of the previous year:

$$282.5 - 260.5 = 22$$

$$22 \;/\; 260.5 = .08$$

Inflation was 8 percent: every dollar of 1982 income was worth only 92¢ of every 1981 dollar. By multiplying the 1982 per capita income by 92 percent, you can calculate the increase or decrease in real dollars from 1981 to 1982:

$$\$7.60 \times .92 = \$6.99$$

$$\$6.99 \;/\; \$7.40 = .94$$

Thus the income appropriated in 1982/83 is worth 94 percent of that appropriated during 1981. In this hypothetical situation, there has been a 6 percent decrease in real purchasing power, even though there has been a 3 percent increase in dollar per capita support. (Figure 3 and exercises 5 and 6 will help you understand these calculations.)

EXPENDITURES

For each of your budgeted line items (salaries, materials and supplies, capital outlay, etc.), identify the percentage of total expenditures annually and over a five-year period. Compare these trends with the

4. U.S. Department of Labor, Bureau of Labor Statistics, *CPI Detailed Report.*

	1978	1979	1980	1981	1982
Income, by source					
Local	___	___	___	___	___
State	___	___	___	___	___
Federal	___	___	___	___	___
Gifts	___	___	___	___	___
Other	___	___	___	___	___
Total	___	___	___	___	___
Total income per capita	___	___	___	___	___
Expenditure, by category					
Personal services	___	___	___	___	___
Benefits	___	___	___	___	___
Materials & supplies	___	___	___	___	___
Capital outlay	___	___	___	___	___
Total	___	___	___	___	___
Registered borrowers					
Adult	___	___	___	___	___
Juvenile	___	___	___	___	___
Total	___	___	___	___	___
Percent of total population	___	___	___	___	___
Circulation of materials					
Adult	___	___	___	___	___
Juvenile	___	___	___	___	___
Total	___	___	___	___	___
Total circ. per capita	___	___	___	___	___
Total circ. per registered borrower	___	___	___	___	___
Total circ. per volume	___	___	___	___	___
OR					
Circulation of materials					
Print materials	___	___	___	___	___
Nonprint materials	___	___	___	___	___
Total	___	___	___	___	___
Volumes, beginning of year					
Total	___	___	___	___	___
Added	___	___	___	___	___
Weeded	___	___	___	___	___
Volumes, end of year					
Adult	___	___	___	___	___
Juvenile	___	___	___	___	___
Total	___	___	___	___	___
Titles, end of year					
Adult	___	___	___	___	___
Juvenile	___	___	___	___	___
Total	___	___	___	___	___
Titles per capita	___	___	___	___	___

Figure 2. Five-Year Analysis of Data

dollar trends in figure 2, and also your knowledge of the library's emphases. Do your rising personnel and utility costs reflect the library's priorities? Are there other substantial changes?

	1978	1979	1980	1981	1982
Magazine subscriptions					
Total, end of year	___	___	___	___	___
Nonprint items, end of year					
Recordings	___	___	___	___	___
Cassettes	___	___	___	___	___
Films	___	___	___	___	___
Filmstrips	___	___	___	___	___
Software	___	___	___	___	___
Other	___	___	___	___	___
Total	___	___	___	___	___
Reference questions					
Walk-in patrons	___	___	___	___	___
Telephone	___	___	___	___	___
Mail	___	___	___	___	___
OR					
Information services					
Reference questions	___	___	___	___	___
Directional transactions	___	___	___	___	___
Interlibrary loan					
Items loaned to systems	___	___	___	___	___
Items loaned to networks	___	___	___	___	___
Items loaned to other agencies	___	___	___	___	___
Total loaned	___	___	___	___	___
Total requests received	___	___	___	___	___
Items borrowed from systems	___	___	___	___	___
Items borrowed from networks	___	___	___	___	___
Items borrowed from others	___	___	___	___	___
Total items borrowed	___	___	___	___	___
Total requests received	___	___	___	___	___
Outreach					
Adult programs	___	___	___	___	___
Juvenile programs	___	___	___	___	___
Total	___	___	___	___	___
Adult attendance	___	___	___	___	___
Juvenile attendance	___	___	___	___	___
Total	___	___	___	___	___
Out-of-library programs					
Total	___	___	___	___	___

Figure 2. Continued

NUMBER OF REGISTERED BORROWERS

What does it mean to have 2,000 people registered? Nothing at all, until you calculate your registrants as a percentage of the community's population. Two thousand registered borrowers are 80 percent

Year	Total Income	Per Capita Income	Percent of Change	CPI at Midyear	Percent of Real-Dollar Increase or Decrease
1977	_____	_____		_____	
1978	_____	_____	_____	_____	_____
1979	_____	_____	_____	_____	_____
1980	_____	_____	_____	_____	_____
1981	_____	_____	_____	_____	_____
1982	_____	_____	_____	_____	_____

Figure 3. Calculating Real-Income Changes

of a population of 2,500, and only 2 percent of 100,000. By using population data from figure 1 and statistics on registered borrowers from figure 2, you can make this calculation easily and include it in figure 2 as well.

Even 2 percent of the population may be significant if that number represents an increase from the year before. The increase is calculated by dividing the number of registrants during the current year by the number of registrants last year (in this example, 1,500), then subtracting 1.

$$2,000 / 1,500 = 1.33$$

$$1.33 - 1 = .33$$

This is a 33 percent increase in registrations.

CIRCULATION

Your circulation figures can be analyzed by type of materials (print or nonprint) or by type of borrower (adult or juvenile). Changes in circulation may clue you in to changing expectations of the library's users.

By dividing the total circulation by the total number of items in the collection, you can get an average annual circulation per item held. This "turnover" rate of materials can be further divided into print and nonprint.

INFORMATION SERVICES

The number of reference questions should be tallied in a consistent way, either by source (walk-in patron, telephone, mail), by type of question (directional or reference), by length of time it takes to respond (in increments of 5 minutes), or by kind of information sought.

OUTREACH

Keep statistics on the number of programs offered each year, the number of people served, and the percentage of increase or decrease. Information showing the growing number of people benefiting from your outreach activities will be of interest to your finance committee when you approach it for additional support. A decreasing demand will support your decision to curtail or drop some outreach services.

FACILITIES

On the maps of census tracts, pinpoint the location of each of the library's service facilities. What can you learn from studying the physical area surrounding them? Perhaps there is a large highway or a railroad yard separating the library from some of your prospective clientele. This may give you insight into the reason so few youngsters seem to come from that side of the city.

COOPERATIVE ACTIVITIES

Borrowing and lending materials at patrons' requests are important elements in your information service. Keep statistics on the percentage of total requests unfilled and of those filled within the system, by a network, and by other resources. Keep the same kind of data for the materials loaned from your library to others in the system, to networks, and to other agencies.

By using the information you gather for the community survey (population characteristics and description of the environment) with the library statistics you are keeping, you are closer to being able to develop a statement about the library's role in the community. You now have to measure the performance of library services currently offered.

Library Performance

Finally, you must determine measures of performance like those suggested by Palmour, Bellassai, and DeWath. These have been tried and tested and can be used in any library. You will need more information about use of the collection, facilities, and staff for making these measurements.

By choosing three days in a week which represent high, medium, and low use, or by using one full week,[5] you can gather data through patron observation on

> building use
> use of materials inside the building
> use of materials outside the building
> characteristics of users
> use of reference services
> activities of public service personnel

The following descriptions do not prescribe a program for measuring performance, but are aimed at indicating some of the areas studied and the kinds of things learned in a performance measurement. For details, see *A Planning Process*, and also *Performance Measures for Public Libraries*, by De Prospo, Altman, and Beasley (Chicago: American Library Association, 1973).

During the week of evaluation, as users enter the building, a staff member or volunteer, acting as a monitor, could note the time on a ticket and hand it to each entering patron, asking that questions on it be completed and the ticket returned as the patron leaves the building. The ticket can ask about

> sex
> student/nonstudent
> grade level of student
> occupation of nonstudent
> some question about satisfaction with services

The question about user satisfaction may be general or specifically designed to target areas of library service. For example, ask whether the patron found what he or she was looking for. Then, in a follow-up question, ask for the author and title of anything not found. The library staff can use this information to see whether the library has the material. They can use this information in collection evaluation and evaluation of reader services, etc., since it represents a case of unfulfilled demand.

When the patron returns the ticket, the monitor again notes the time. By multiplying the average length of a library visit by the number of people entering the building, you can determine the total number of hours patrons spent in the library. (Another way to calculate user service hours will be mentioned later.)

5. Palmour, Bellassai, and DeWath, *A Planning Process for Public Libraries* (Chicago: ALA, 1980), pp. 127–128.

Circulation figures do not reflect actual building and collection usage. So, during this three- to five-day sampling period, you can make rounds every 20 minutes, counting the number and types of materials (books, serials, records, pamphlets, microforms) that are used and left on tables. (The latter are reshelved before the next count, of course.) By keeping separate records for juvenile and adult items, by noting types of materials and the time of day, you can estimate the proportion of in-house use by type of material, kind of user, and time of use.

When charging materials out of the library, you can count the number of borrowers at the different times of day. This gives you the opportunity to calculate the percentage of persons who borrow materials, the average number of items borrowed per person, and the circulation per day and hour. You might also want to calculate annual circulation per capita, per registered borrower, and per title or per volume held.

Count the number of seats and equipment, such as record players, microform readers, photocopiers, audio and visual equipment, and meeting rooms. Then, during your 20-minute rounds, record what facilities are used, by whom, and at what time of day. Figure 4 may be useful.

User service hours are also measured by projecting, from your 20-minute rounds, the average number of patrons who use the library each hour and multiplying that figure by the number of hours the library is open. These data may have implications for deciding the hours of service and the kind of staff on duty at different times.

Patterns of reference use can be determined by keeping statistics during the trial period:

> When was the question asked?
> Was it directional or source related?   .
> If source related, what sources were used?
> Was it asked by an adult, student, or someone from another library?
> Was it asked in person, over the telephone, or by mail?
> Was it successfully answered?

These data will be used to consider reference activity, staffing patterns, and selection of reference materials.

The availability and use of staff are also measures of library performance. The schedules of staff members could be analyzed to determine the number assigned to each public area and the number available on the floor.

	Books	Magazines	Records	Pamphlets	Microforms	Seats	Photocopier	AV Equipment	Meeting Rooms	Microform Readers
Time										
Number used by adults										
Number used by children										
Time										
Number used by adults										
Number used by children										
Time										
Number used by adults										
Number used by children										

Figure 4. Use of Library Facilities

Through observation and reference statistics, you can determine the number of staff who serve patrons at any time. These data allow you to calculate the percent of assigned staff who are available, the percentage available and assisting someone, and the percentage available but not assisting anyone at various times.

Now What?

You now have a community profile, an annual and five-year analysis of library statistics, and measures of library performance. Pulling the supporting data together is time consuming. Once done, however, the community profile may not have to be revised until new census data are available. The five-year analysis of library statistics need only be kept up to date. You may want to measure performance in selected areas to monitor and evaluate any program changes you make. Use this information as support data to define your library's role in the community.

Role or mission statements will vary. A school library may limit itself to informational and educational activities, while a public library may also try to meet cultural and recreational needs. A school librarian may address information services and materials, while a public library may add programming and outreach. Again, a school library may limit its clientele to its students and teachers, while a public library may define its constituency as adults, young adults, children, senior citizens, minorities, handicapped, unemployed, and so forth.

The first thing to do is review any existing library mission or goal statements. Too often, goal statements have been developed as a response to organizational pressures without reference to any objective data. They sound good, but may not be effective for library planning. Ask yourself some questions as you review them.

> Do these goal statements provide the scope necessary to cover the broad purpose of the library?
>
> Are they specific enough to provide direction for program planning?
>
> Are they supported by the data collected in the community profile, the library's statistics and measures of performance?
>
> Do they need to be changed to accomplish any or all of the three questions above?

To help you answer the last question, you might use a checklist like the one suggested by Palmour, Bellassai, and DeWath.[6] The

6. Ibid., p. 54.

checklist, which must be tailored to the library and its community, can be used to stimulate discussion among staff and board members or school administration as they compare the point spread each has assigned to the areas of activity, service, and clientele.

As discussions about the role of your library progress, remember that the role statement should include who is to be served and through what types of service. It may narrate the status quo or it may define changes in direction.

For example, a role statement which continues current services but recognizes new clientele may read:

> "The library will continue to provide educational, informational, and recreational services to all children and adults of the city; and will develop outreach activities for the aging, handicapped, and functionally illiterate adult residents of the city."

A school library which recognizes that there is an accessible public library, well stocked to meet the recreational reading needs of its students, may decide:

> "The library will make available materials supportive of the curriculum to its students and teachers."

Another school library, emphasizing library-use instruction and reference services, may decide:

> "The library will provide information, curriculum-related materials, and instruction in the use of the library to the students and teachers of the school."

Another library, recipient of three computers the year before, reassessed its role when the statistics showed a decline in use of print materials and lines of kids waiting their turn on the computers. After much discussion about the need for computer literacy, the library-use data, and expected revenue, the library staff and school administration agreed

> "To keep the magazine and reference collection current, provide curriculum-related software and develop computer literacy classes for teachers and students."

A change in role as drastic as this cannot be made without assurance of administrative, user, and funding support. That support is more likely to be available when those decisions are based on objective data.

Summary

It is easy to say that libraries exist to provide informational, recreational, educational, and cultural opportunities to their communities. But it is more demanding to say why a particular library exists in a specific community—why it is important and why it should be funded.

To answer this question in a responsible way, you need to gather information about your community, about current library services and the performance of those services. Only then will you have the background information needed to begin discussing the role of the library in the community.

That discussion should include at least the library staff and the board of trustees or the school administration. The discussion allows the staff to think about and understand the importance of their daily work. It provides opportunity for the board or school administration to understand what it will be asked to defend at future budgetary hearings. (This last point cannot be stressed enough.)

Each library will define a different role for itself, one which is tied in with the makeup of its community. From that general, direction-giving role, specific goals and objectives will be developed. This next step is discussed in detail in chapter 2.

PRACTICE EXPERIENCES

1. Locate maps and data on census tracts served by your library or school. If you are not a working librarian, do so for the neighborhood in which you live.

2. Complete the first three columns of figure 1 for the census tract in which your library, school, or home is located.

3. Complete the fourth and fifth columns on figure 1, comparing the 1980 census tract data with the 1980 population characteristics of the community as a whole.

4. If you do not have information regarding library support, assume that the per capita income in 1977 was $5.40 and in 1982, $7.60. Calculate the percentage increase or decrease in per capita support from 1977 to 1982.

5. If you are a librarian, calculate the per capita income for your library each year from 1977 to 1982. Calculate the percentage increase or decrease in per capita support over the five-year period. Complete columns 1, 2, and 3 of figure 3.

6. The CPI in January 1977 was 175.3 and in January 1982, 282.5. Locate the CPI for each of the interim years, then calculate the inflation rate over the five-year period and complete the third and fourth columns of figure 3.

SELECTED READINGS

De Prospo, Ernest R., Ellen Altman, and Kenneth E. Beasley. *Performance Measures for Public Libraries*. Chicago: Public Library Association, ALA. 1973.

Palmour, Vernon E., Marcia C. Bellassai, and Nancy V. DeWath. *A Planning Process for Public Libraries*. Chicago: ALA, 1980.

2
Program Budgeting for Ultimate Success

One of the significant questions which must be resolved when you begin the budgeting process is where to start. What will be the basis for organizing your efforts? How will you begin? What steps must be taken to develop a defensible, realistic budget to present to your funding agency?

Often librarians and other managers begin by looking back at the budgets of preceding budget years to determine what *has* been done. This is a positive way to begin, for it provides a sense of the budgetary history of the organization.

However, once some very basic observations have been made about those previous years' budgets, the first question comes back again: What will be the basis of my budgeting efforts? Most budgets which you will encounter are in what is commonly described as *line-item format,* in which expenditures are categorized according to kinds of things and services purchased, regardless of how they are used by the library. They may puzzle the inexperienced manager/librarian, for many of the line items do not effectively identify what has actually happened in the library in those previous years.

What is needed in the budget is some method of identifying what is going on, what is being accomplished, how the use of money achieves outcomes, how the role of the library is carried out in the community. The process which will be described in this chapter will assist you in dealing with many of these fundamental budgeting questions. At the end of the chapter you will also find an example of how the program budgeting process may be put to work to deal with such issues. With these ideas in mind, let's explore the elements of what is commonly called *program budgeting*.

Program budgets relate the expenditures of the library to the services they provide. Programs are usually defined by the common library functions of administration, acquisitions, processing, etc. However, programs may alternatively be defined by clientele served or by service units. In general, the aim of the program budget is to show how much the library spends on each of its various services.

In contrast, the line-item budget shows what the library spends on the goods and services it acquires. Instead of being organized by programs, this commonly used budget format is organized by categories of items bought: personal services, materials and supplies, capital outlay, purchased services, etc.

The line-item format is incorporated into the program budget format, as indicated in figure 5. By identifying expenditure categories for each program, you end with miniline-item budgets which can then be compiled and transferred into either a comprehensive line-item budget or a program budget. Even if your final budget must be in the line-item format, it is easier to make service-related changes if it is built from the program budget approach.

Program budgets look like minibudgets which support each of the library's identified activities. Each has line-item amounts, focused on the resources needed to achieve the goals of every program/function of the library.

Figure 5 indicates how these concepts of line items and programs are related in the program budget format. As you see, each program/function will include many line items. Every line item is usually needed for every program/function. The lines on the chart represent a few

Line Items	Programs/Functions				
	Acquisitions	Processing	Circulation	Reference	Etc.
Personnel					
Employee benefits					
Materials & supplies					
Purchased services					
Etc.					

Figure 5. Basic Program Budget

that usually are found in a completed line-item budget. The programs/ functions also are representative of those which may ultimately be included in a complete program budget. Detailed descriptions of line-item budgeting and expenditure projection follow in chapters 3–5.

Program budgeting is stressed in this text because it offers a number of managerial advantages:

> It coordinates with the library's planning process.
> It identifies money spent on the activities stressed by the library's role statements.
> If there is a gap between current and desired service levels, the program budgeting process helps you decide how best to meet those needs.
> It offers you a management tool helpful in making service-related changes.

The program budgeting process is carried out in six basic steps:

> Identify the programs (also called *activity centers* and *functions*) and their goals. The goals should be clearly related to the library's role statement which was developed during the planning process.
> Project changes in each program for the coming year by setting objectives to meet the goals of each program, evaluating alternative ways of meeting the objectives and selecting the ways to meet them.
> Prepare a line-item budget for each program.
> Rank the programs by order of importance, according to their relevance to the library's role in the community.
> Compile the budgets of the programs into the final program budget for the entire library.
> Evaluate both the budgeting process and whether the funded programs accomplished their established objectives.

Identifying Programs

A program is a focus of organizational activity which can be separately defined and for which a specific set of goals and objectives can be developed. The programs identified are somewhat different in every organization. The pattern used in this chapter is merely illustrative, and you should not use it without modification. Your library setting may be different enough to justify a unique approach. For instance, the very differences in the structure of an organization will have some impact on the way program categories might be identified. A public library would develop program categories different from a school library. The issue is to study carefully the functions of the library for which the budget is being developed, and list each of these as possible "program" categories.

Establishing the basis on which programs are defined is critical to the entire process. Programs are usually defined by the functions the library staff perform: administration, acquisitions, technical processing, circulation, and reference. They can also be defined by the clientele served: adult, young adult, and children's services; outreach to community groups; and service to business. Still another way to define programs is by service centers, that is, branches, bookmobiles and deposit collections, and main-library services. In every case, there should be a direct link between the library's role statement and its programs.

If programs are not clearly defined, program results cannot be clearly described. Lack of clarity in program identification may cause confusion and misdirection of resources. Ultimately, the final evaluations will not identify real program achievements. Accurate program identification leads to clear objectives and evaluations. It allows you to communicate results easily understood by your parent agency and the general public as well.

HOW TO IDENTIFY YOUR PROGRAMS

A procedure to follow to identify programs is to identify and list functions of the library. Ask your staff to do the same independently. Then collect all the lists and post the item on a large wallboard so that everyone can add whatever he or she thinks necessary.

Example A: Functions of the Library
> Buy books
> Circulate materials
> Teach people to use the card catalog
> Answer reference questions
> Cataloging and classification
> Ordering materials
> Cleaning the building
> Story hours
> Exhibits
> Crafts programs
> Place to study
> An escape from home

Attend meetings and watch movies
Shelving and redoing shelves
Weeding
Getting back issues of magazines people ask for
Overdues
Interlibrary loans

Compare the results of your planning documents with the functions listed on the wallchart. Continue to combine, compile, and refine these categories until you think you have considered them all.
Assume the role statement reads:

"The library will continue to provide educational, informational, and recreational services to all children and adults of the city, and will develop outreach activities for the aging, handicapped, and functionally illiterate adult residents of the city."

This might result in an outcome as follows.

Example B: Functions of the Library
Educational services to adults and children
Informational services to adults and children
Recreational services to adults and children
Outreach to:
    Handicapped
    Senior citizens
    Functionally illiterate adults

Group ideas into the smallest, most closely related functions. These become your major program budget categories. In a public library with the above role statement, the programs may then be identified as follows.

Example C: Functions of the Library
Administration
Outreach
Collections, Adult
Collections, Children
Information
Circulation, Adult
Circulation, Children
Programming, Adult
Programming, Children

FROM PROGRAMS TO GOALS

Write a brief statement of an achievable goal for each program. While writing your statements, you may discover that some programs need to be further divided for clarity, combined with some other activity center, or deleted as not feasible. Make sure that all functions of the library are included within some program category.

An appropriate goal statement for the outreach program might be:

> "The library will develop, within this fiscal year, special responses to the identified needs for outreach activities to (1) the aging, (2) the handicapped, and (3) the functionally illiterate adult residents of the city."

This goal statement takes a part of the library's role statement and gives it focus for the current year.

This focus will be further refined by developing objectives, stated in accomplishable and measurable ways. Goals provide the intermediate focus of each program or activity center. They are usually applied to the program in a way which will make it possible to develop appropriate objectives. However, goal statements are general in nature, and are not stated in measurable terms. That is, they cannot, without their objectives, be evaluated in terms of their accomplishment.

Let's look at the adult circulation program identified earlier. A goal statement within that program might read:

> "Materials will be shelved promptly to provide for maximum accessibility."

As will be seen in the next section, this goal statement can facilitate the development of objectives for the adult circulation program.

The purpose of writing program goals is to interpret the data gathered during the planning process and relate them to the program's response to those needs. The goal can call for the continuation of activities or for changes to address discrepancies which have been identified through the data developed in the planning process.

Developing Objectives to Project Changes

Achievability is critical in setting program goals and objectives. Your payoff is the ease with which you can evaluate each program. Let's look at this problem from the perspective of the funding board. It's easy to imagine some member saying, "If you want to achieve these goals, we'll give you the needed funds. But we must know what you'll accomplish at each stage of the program."

Your first step is to ask yourself a few questions:

> What do you expect each program to accomplish during the budget year?
> What "time lines" for services must you meet?
> What tasks must you complete?
> What quality of service will be acceptable to you?

WRITING OBJECTIVES FOR PROGRAM BUDGETS

Most objectives are written in a format developed by Robert Mager. In his format, the objective has three parts:

> What are you going to accomplish?
> How are you going to accomplish it?
> How can you tell when you have accomplished it?

As a school librarian, you are called upon to teach students how to use the library—a demand especially frequent at the beginning of the school year. Your objective might be to meet 90 percent of the demand by (a) extending the library's hours during the first month of the school year or (b) organizing a group of library volunteers to lead the classes in order to meet 90 percent of the demand during the first month of the school year. The change in this case is in the "how" of meeting the expected level of accomplishment.

Let's look at another example. You're evaluating the goal of your circulation program, which is to maximize accessibility through prompt shelving of materials. During the past year the employees of several new companies in your town have increased the demand on library circulation. These pressures have resulted in two major problems:

> Lines at the checkout counter
> Piles of unshelved materials

This is an increasing problem you must consider in your program budget for circulation. How are you to proceed?

You'll formulate an objective to help define what you plan to accomplish, how you plan to accomplish it, and how you can tell when it has been accomplished. In this case, your plan is to decrease the delays in checking out and reshelving materials. Using statistics and data collected about your library's performance, you might come up with a number of options.

Alternative A: Reschedule your staff according to library performance data.

Alternative B: Budget added staff to check out and reshelve
materials faster.

Alternative C: Ask a library volunteer to check out and reshelve materials.

Alternative D: Do nothing about the problem.

How will you know when your objectives have been satisfactorily
accomplished? How will you evaluate your efforts? You could decide
to:

Allow patrons to wait no longer than 4 minutes in checkout
lines.

Reshelve all materials twice each day.

Allow no more than 10 items to accumulate.

Reshelve all overnight returns within the first 3 hours the
library is open.

Expect these high levels of performance 90 percent of the
time.

Why 90 percent of the time? It would be unrealistic to set a goal
of 100 percent if its accomplishment would require all your staff to
be present all the time. You cannot set a standard too low, either,
since it might result in criticism of the library management. You
must set an *acceptable* level of accomplishment; or you might find
yourself defending an attempt to accomplish the impossible, which
could undermine your credibility and that of your staff.

EVALUATION OF ALTERNATIVES

Alternative A involves no additional cost. Staff reshuffling, however,
could present problems in morale. You could reduce the impact of
this problem by discussing slack time and work priorities with each
of them and involving them in working out ways to implement this
alternative.

Alternative B results in changing the *personnel* and *employee benefits*
line items in the circulation minibudget. If the hourly wage is $3.50,
the annual cost of adding just one hour a day of staff time would be
$910 ($3.50 × 260 working days = $910). You can determine the
number of hours actually needed by reviewing your library performance (so many items reshelved per hour) and comparing this with
the average number of items to be reshelved over a two-week period.
If employee benefits are required, the appropriate percentage of

wages would be applied to the $910 and placed in the employee-benefits line item.

Alternative C calls for no additional cost; but someone on your staff will have to recruit and train volunteers. If a volunteer training program doesn't exist, you'll have to develop one. Because the turn-over of volunteers is expected to be high, you might need to adjust the 90 percent expectation downward.

Alternative D would leave the situation as it is. You might decide that this need is not worth pursuing.

As a manager, you face the decision of assessing the critical nature of the need and probability of implementing one of the alternatives. Your decision is based on the relationship of *cost* to *effectiveness*. That is, are the costs worth the results? Will the difference be significant? Is this difference critical to accomplishment of the objective?

Using our example, you decide to pursue the situation without additional funds, and knowing that volunteers will probably be too demanding of staff time, you call your staff together to work out a reshuffling of assignments. In your judgment, alternative A is the most cost effective for achieving the objective. It adds no cost to the program budget and will be viewed positively by most funding agencies as wise decision making and wise management.

Completing the Program Budgets

When you have written objectives for each of the library's programs, you can summarize their costs by using a separate sheet (like figures 6 and 7) for each objective and each program.

Occasionally, there is only one legitimate method of achieving an objective; more often, there will be more. Having identified these,

Program: Circulation

Objectives	Alternative Methods of Achieving Objective	Estimated Cost
1. Reshelve all over-night returns within first 3 hours of busi-ness	1a. Reschedule staff	1a. None
	1b. Add 1 hour per day of staff time	1b. $910 plus benefits
	1c. Use volunteers	1c. None
	1d. Do nothing	1d. None

Figure 6. Alternatives for Program Budgeting: Circulation

Program: Instruction

Objectives	Alternative Methods of Achieving Objective	Estimated Cost
1. Meet 90% of skills-training demand in first month of school	1a. Train volunteers to teach library skills 1b. Extend library hours during first month of school: 1 hour per day for librarian and clerk for 20 days	1a. None 1b. Librarian: $14 × 20 = $280 Clerk: $ 4 × 20 = $ 80 Total $360

Figure 7. Alternatives for Program Budgeting: Instruction

Program: Circulation

Items	Objectives					
	1	2	3	4	5	...
Personnel						
Employee benefits						
Travel						
Purchased services						
Supplies						
Books						
...						
Total						

Figure 8. Program Budget Sheet: Circulation

you will decide which alternatives can provide the most effective and efficient investment of your library's dollars.

COMPILE THE MINIBUDGETS

Now we are ready to produce the minibudgets. The process is simplified since the cost of each of the most effective alternatives can now be placed on the program budget sheet (figure 8). These are then added to provide the line-item amounts on each line for the program.

RANKING PROGRAMS AND ESTABLISHING PRIORITIES

When all the minibudgets have been developed, you're ready to establish program priorities—a necessary step because your budget need will almost always exceed your expected appropriations.

Since some needs must be placed on more than a one-year time frame, priorities are usually set for activities of subsequent years as well as for the current year. Several activities occur every year, such as administration, circulation, processing, and acquisitions. Others, like the development and construction of a new library, may be partly carried out during any given year.

The program objectives, alternatives, and their costs (as developed in figures 6 and 7) will be invaluable tools for this exercise. You can review the objectives and the cost of alternative methods of achievement to determine the most efficient cost tradeoffs. The goal is to achieve the maximum library effectiveness within the funds available. To do this:

> Identify programs without which the library would cease to function (e.g., acquisitions, a service center, information).
> List the less critical programs, until all programs are ranked according to priority.
> Have your library staff make independent rankings.
> Compile and compare the lists.
> Obtain agreement on priority rankings.
> Compile final budget totals.

Figure 9 indicates a final program budget recap sheet. All developmental materials leading to it become back-up documents which will help guide you through the budgeting process and the budget year.

Evaluating the Process

The next-to-the-last step of program budgeting is evaluating the process used for developing the minibudgets. Called *process evaluation*, it seeks to answer such questions as

> Are budget-development time lines being met?
> Are all elements in the budgeting process being accomplished in an appropriate manner?
> Are the necessary people involved in the budgetary process?
> Is the scope of the budgeting process adequate to accomplish the expected results?

Library Programs	Personnel	Employee Benefits	Travel	Purchased Services	Supplies	Books	...	...	Objective Total	Program Total
Program: _____										
Objective 1										
Objective 2										
Objective 3										
Objective . . .										
Program: _____										
Objective 1										
Objective 2										
Objective 3										
Objective . . .										
Program: _____										
Objective 1										
Objective . . .										
Line-Item Totals										

Figure 9. Program Budget with Detailed Objectives

Are budget data being gathered about the accomplishment of objectives?

Are staff members aware of their part in the budget-data gathering?

Are the appropriate forms ready when needed to gather data?

Is the data gathering sufficient for the scope of the objectives?

If any of these questions is answered contrary to the intent of the objectives, you can make corrections while the process is taking place. For instance, if the time lines for the year are not being met, determine why and adjust either the timing or the process.

Evaluating Results

The final step is *product evaluation*. In this step, the effectiveness of the budget in managing the library is evaluated. It answers questions such as:

Were the objectives accomplished?

How should the information be organized for presentation?

To whom should it be presented?

There is no general formula or chart you can use to summarize the accomplishment of your objectives. Each objective has its own evaluator, built into it. For instance, the higher expectations of reshelving will be maintained 90 percent of the time, and 90 percent of the demand for skills training will be met during the first month of school. Data will be gathered and compared to the standards to determine whether the objectives have been accomplished.

If they have, you'll have reason to refer to them in the next budget proposal process. If they haven't, you must learn why. Was the standard too high? Was the objective possible? Did other factors interfere with success? Should you renew the objective another year?

Feed these answers into your needs assessment as you prepare for next year's budget. If the initial objectives were reasonably well developed and you managed the library well, most of your standards will have been met. If not, use the experience and information as part of next year's budget proposal to improve your record. Developing the budget and its supporting objectives is not easy, but it won't take as long as you may think. As you become more proficient, you'll be able to represent your library, its needs, and programs more effectively each year.

Making the Most of Evaluative Information

As a result of both process and product evaluations, the data

Become input to the subsequent year's planning cycle.
Help in making calculated changes in programs and processes.
Alert funding sources to potential problem areas.
Reassure funding sources about the effective and efficient use of funds.

You'll rarely be satisfied that you've written all your objectives carefully enough or that you've thought about all alternatives. Despite any dissatisfaction you may feel, when the budget year begins, you'll have use for everything you've prepared.

After the first year of program budgeting, it will become easier to budget for the ensuing years because you have established a pattern. You shouldn't have to revise program categories unless the organization undergoes substantial changes or you find that the first year's categories are inadequate.

The main thing is not to be discouraged. The knowledge you've gained will help you detect and correct any errors you may have made. You're now ready to prepare *next* year's budget.

Remember how budgeting cycles overlap. As you put one budget into practice, you'll automatically begin preparing the next one.

Summarizing the Process

Let's summarize the process of program budgeting (figure 10).

Assess needs and planning. Described in chapter 1, this activity establishes the data base for detailing the program budget. It is the reference source of information which leads to the goals and objectives for each identified program area.
Identify programs. This process establishes the scope of library activities and the closely related groupings of these activities, providing the framework into which the budgeting activities will take place.
Develop goals and objectives. Each program category has purposes. The goals and objectives detail these purposes and the actions which will accomplish them.

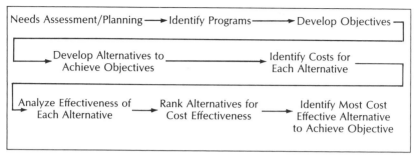

Figure 10. The Process of Program Budgeting

Develop alternatives. Most objectives can be accomplished in several ways, and alternatives provide a basis for identifying the money to be spent in their accomplishment.

Identify costs for each alternative. Identification of costs provides the building blocks of the program budget process. Details are critical at this level.

Analyze effectiveness of each alternative. You, as library manager, must decide the extent to which the various alternatives will accomplish the objectives. As you gather experience in managing, this task becomes somewhat easier.

Rank alternatives for cost effectiveness. Your professional judgment and knowledge of the organization are important here. You decide, given the costs of the alternatives and the extent to which the objective will be accomplished by each, which alternative has the best "balance" between investment of resources and getting the job done.

Identify the most cost effective alternative. After the alternatives are ranked, the final step is to place the best one on the worksheet for inclusion in the budget for a specific program.

Rank the programs in priority. Rank the programs in order of their significance in assisting the library to achieve its overall role in the community—from the most critically important to the least significant. This step also requires weighing their political significance.

Evaluate the process and accomplishment of objectives. The final step in the program budgeting cycle is to evaluate what has been accomplished. Look to the standards established in each objective in each program and evaluate the levels of accomplishment. Feed this information into your planning for the subsequent fiscal year's budget.

The Advantages of Program Budgeting

Program budgets offer an excellent management tool. With them,

> You can evaluate your achievements, since costs are tied to results. (For instance, if your objective is to increase your collection by 5 percent, the cost is related to the increase in the minibudget for acquisitions.) Program budgets require that you identify expected results of programs and the format of the process simplifies evaluation.
> You can direct and control your operation with ease. Programs define specific uses of funds. Therefore you can change program priorities and objectives quickly and easily in the face of budgetary adjustments.
> You can identify the expenditures of each activity center.
> You work with manageable budgeting units. It is often difficult to conceptualize and analyze the changing needs of an entire library, but much easier to analyze the changing needs of smaller units. These latter become the blocks from which the total budget is built.
> A description of library functions is obtained. The format requires that funds be identified with the functions of the library.
> Program budgets make the elements of line-item budgeting simple. Each minibudget maintains line-item identification of funds. Therefore even the line-item budget becomes more manageable.
> Approval of the goals and objectives occurs during the program budgeting process. Fewer misunderstandings about purpose result when funding boards understand what services they are supporting.

If your plans have been effective, you can monitor the progress of the library. You will be able to answer the funding board member who asks: "What will you accomplish at each stage of the program?"

Example of Program Budgeting in Action

Now that you have studied the processes in program budgeting, let's look at how they could be applied in a real situation. This will help as you design applications in your library (and as you work the assignments at the end of this chapter).

Several approaches to program budgeting in this example illustrate that there are no "right" or "wrong" ways to develop the program budget. Sometimes a simpler solution is advisable, and sometimes a more complex approach is called for. The question is whether the resulting budget, which is to be proposed to and approved by the parent organization, is effective. That can never be fully known until approval is obtained and the budget is expended during the operational year.

THE SETTING

Midtown's population is 50,000. It has a central library of 100,000 volumes, serviced by a staff of 13: 7 professional librarians, 1 custodian, and 5 full-time clerical personnel. Two of the professional librarians are reference librarians. The library budget for the current year is $380,000. Library hours are 9 a.m. to 9 p.m. weekdays, 9 a.m. to 5 p.m. Saturday, and noon to 5 p.m. Sunday. Circulation is 2,000 items a week. The library is equipped with a microfiche reader, a microfilm reader and a copy machine, a record and cassette player, and a record and cassette collection. Ten percent of the population of Midtown are registered library borrowers.

Activities of the library include a large children's program, an interlibrary loan program, and outreach programs in different parts of the city: deposit collection, programs for senior citizens, programs at a retarded young adults' center, and an adult literacy program.

The town is beginning to experience growing pains, in the form of 10 percent growth in the past three years. Two large industries are relocating plants into the area and over a five-year period expect to add significantly to the population of the area, providing 1,000 new jobs.

The library has several problems which need to be addressed in planning and budgeting for the subsequent year. The two reference librarians have seen a substantial reduction in usage and now handle only about 20 inquiries per week. The new industries are making it known that they expect trade journals and reference materials to be provided which relate to their special focus and will be of particular interest to their employees.

The young-family population has shifted from the traditional south side to the new housing being developed outside the town limits on the north side. Elderly population concentration is increasing, due to development of a major retirement village in the old southside community, where urban renewal funds have been used extensively by the town council.

The library is operated as a program of the municipality of Midtown and must present its needs each year, along with the other agencies of the town government: the hospital, parks and recreation, police and fire departments, municipal courts, city utilities, the road department, and so forth.

APPLYING THE EXAMPLE

For this example, we assume the identification of the following activity centers for the library:

> Administration
> Outreach
> Collections, Adult
> Collections, Children
> Information
> Circulation, Adult
> Circulation, Children
> Programming, Adult
> Programming, Children

This, of course, is a simplified way of identifying the "activity centers." Initially, as you work with program budgets, it is well to keep it simple. Obviously, many of these activity centers could be broken down into smaller areas.

OUTREACH AS A SINGLE ACTIVITY CENTER

In outreach, each of the special activities could be made into a separate activity center and could be budgeted separately. Or they could all be budgeted together, under the outreach label, as a single activity center. The decision is usually determined by how they are managed: if together, in a single structure, they are budgeted as a single program; if separate, they are budgeted separately. In this case, due to the size of the library operation and its management, it has been decided to budget them as a single center.

After we have identified the activity center (the programs of the program budget), the next step is to develop the objectives. The goal of outreach in this example is to extend the services and activities of the library into the community to make these services and activities more accessible to library patrons.

The objectives could include the following:

> 1. Sustain current year's service level of the outreach activity center through the new budget year by providing the same staffing and operating levels.

2. Meet half of the demand for technical books and periodicals exerted by the new-industry residents.
3. Establish a circulation center at the senior citizens' complex not later than December 1.
4. Conduct a needs assessment of persons at the Retarded Young Adult Center by January 30.
5. Analyze demographic characteristics of participants in the adult literacy program by conducting a voluntary survey of the first fall-class meetings. The results will be compared with the current program to determine appropriateness of location and times.

Notice that these objectives are written in a form to simplify their evaluation. Objectives 1, 3, 4, and 5 are evaluated by accomplishing the stated tasks (i.e., Has the same level of staffing and operation been sustained? Was a circulation center established not later than December 1? Was the needs assessment conducted and completed by January 30? Was the analysis of demographic characteristics carried out and the comparison accomplished?) For objective 2, the new demand could be identified by analyzing requests by new-industry residents over a given period of time. Then the extent to which these demands could be met through interlibrary loans would be analyzed. This would establish whether half the demand had been met.

These represent major objectives for the outreach activity center and suggest that the outreach program is spread among various areas. A baseline is provided through objective 1, indicating that this year's level of service has been satisfactory. If this were the first year to have program objectives, a rather complete description of services (spelled out through such objectives) would have to be developed. It is usually more effective to keep these in broader (rather than narrow) scope to cover the major purposes for which the program exists; otherwise a large number of objectives would result, and the sheer weight of them becomes oppressive.

For instance, an objective for the previous year might have been "establish contact with the Retarded Young Adult Center to determine if its library needs are being met." The "contact" could be in the form of a luncheon with the director, to establish rapport, and a subsequent visit to the home. This year's objective 4 would then be logical. However, objective 1 indicates that current activities will be continued, including the luncheon with the director and visits.

According to figure 10, the next steps are to

| Develop Alternatives to
Achieve Objectives | ⟶ | Identify Costs for
Each Alternative |

Thus two items in your budgeting documentation might look like figure 11.

The next steps in the process are:

Analyze Effectiveness
of ──────▶
Each Alternative

Rank Alternatives for
Cost ──────▶
Effectiveness

Identify Most Cost
Effective Alternative
to Achieve Objective

For objective 2, you would proceed as follows. The cost for alternative A is predicted to be $300, to cover postage. (You have estimated that the additional daily burden on the staff will not be noticeable.) The cost of alternative C would be 1/2 hour per day of clerical time plus benefits, and approximately $1,000 for acquisitions. Alternative B costs the same as A, the difference being in how the objective might best be accomplished. This depends on the supply of technical books in the state library and the feasibility of establishing an agreement with the technical school.

Nothing would prevent you from adopting both of these alternatives, if both could be worked out. Your initial reaction to the comparison of A and C is that A is more cost effective than C. However, a key issue is whether this is true only in the short run, or would also be true in the long run. Let's look at the long-run economics (figure 12), using a five-year period of time (on the assumption that within 5 years materials in a technical field have changed sufficiently to require repurchase). Thus is appears that alternative A is meeting the objective.

Perhaps there are other factors to be considered.

1. What is the merit of having the books in the collection, as opposed to the delay in interlibrary loans?
2. Can technical books be obtained through interlibrary loan agreements with either the state library or a technical school?
3. Would purchased technical books go out of date quickly (due to changes in technology), resulting in the need to repurchase before the end of the five-year period?
4. Is expenditure for acquisitions justified by the numbers of potential clientele?

Your answers to these (and other) questions may provide pertinent issues to consider in making your decisions about the benefits of cost efficiency compared with overall effectiveness. You may determine that technical books indeed go out of date quickly, due to advances

Program Outreach

Objective	Alternative Method of Achieving Objective	Cost Estimates
1. To sustain current year's level of service of outreach activity center through new budget year by providing same staffing and operating levels	1a. Maintain staffing at same level 1b. No alternative is available*	1ai. Personnel same, plus 7% raise ii. Employee benefits same, plus 7% raise iii. Supplies same, plus 10% inflation iv. Books/supplies same v. Equipment same
2. To meet half of demand for technical books and periodicals by new-industry residents	2a. Initiate reciprocal borrowing program with a technical-vocational school	2ai. Personnel same ii. Employee benefits same iii. Supplies (postage) will increase $300 iv. Books/periodicals same v. Equipment same
	2b. Increase state library interlibrary loan	2b. Same as 2a costs
	2c. Purchase additional books for collection (Transfer to acquisitions activity center if this is preferred alternative)	2ci. Personnel increase ½ hr. per day, clerical time ii. Employee benefits change to cover ½ hr. per day clerical time iii. Supplies same iv. Books/periodicals increase by 50 at $20 each v. Equipment same

*This sometimes happens. The objective was stated in such a way as to provide for no alternatives.

Figure 11. Listing Alternatives for an Outreach Program

in a field. You also discover that the cost of such books is at least 50 percent higher than other books you usually acquire. Additionally, you determine that a nearby technical school keeps current on such materials and that its collection could become available to you through

Cost of Alternative A		Cost of Alternative C	
1st year	$ 300	1st year	$1,000 book acquisitions
2nd year	300		½ hr. per day @ $4.25/hr.
3rd year	300		X 260 days/year = $552
4th year	300		+ 20% employee benefits
5th year	300		= $110.50
Total	$1,500		Total $1,663
		2nd year	0
		3rd year	0
		4th year	0
		5th year	0
		Total	$1,663

Figure 12. Long-Run (5-Year) Economic Projection

an interlibrary agreement. Therefore the final columns of your document should be as shown in figure 13.

Each of the other objectives listed for the cost center would be extended in the same way. The packages would be summarized on a program budget sheet, similar to figure 14.

Each of these budget sheets would be totaled (like the budget sheet in figure 9).

	Cost Ranking (#1 Least Costly)	Overall Effectiveness (#1 Best)
Alternative 2a	1	1
Alternative 2b	1	2
Alternative 2c	3	3

Alternative 2a is included for placement on your program sheet.

Figure 13. Cost vs. Effectiveness Comparison

Program Outreach	Objective 2	
	Current Year	Proposed Next Year
Personnel	$XX.XX	Same
Employee benefits	$XX.XX	Same
Supplies	$XX.XX	$300
Books/periodicals	$XX.XX	Same
Equipment	$XX.XX	Same

Figure 14. Program Budget Sheet Summary

PRACTICE EXPERIENCES

1. Develop a chart (like the one in example A, page 20) for your library or for the Midtown library example on page 33. Make sure that all major activities are included.

2. For one of the program categories on that chart, develop figure 11 as completely as you can.

3. Design a process and product evaluation process for this category (which you chose in 2 above).

4. From memory, replicate figure 10.

5. Develop a chart (similar to the one in example C, page 21) which lists all the program elements of a library.

6. Identify on that chart the rank order of programs, from the most to the least critical, to form your priority list of programs.

7. Define, in your own words, the two-evaluation processes.

SELECTED READINGS

Bennett, F. Lawrence. *Critical Path Precedence Networks*. New York: Van Nostrand Reinhold, 1977.

Bittel, Lester R., ed. *Encyclopedia of Professional Management*. New York: McGraw-Hill, 1979.

Bloom, Benjamin S., et al. *Taxonomy of Educational Objectives: Handbook I: Cognitive Domain*. New York: Longman, 1977.

Krathwohl, David R. "Stating Objectives Appropriately for Program, for Curriculum, and for Instructional Materials Development." *Journal of Teacher Education* (March 1965), pp.83–92.

———, ed. *Taxonomy of Educational Objectives: Handbook II: Affective Domain*. New York: Longman, 1969.

Lee, Sul H., ed. *Planning-Programming-Budgeting System (PPBS) Implications for Library Management*. Ann Arbor: Pierian, 1973.

Mager, Robert. *Goal Analysis*. Belmont, Calif.: Pitman, 1972.

———. *Preparing Instruction Objectives*. 2nd ed. Belmont, Calif.: Pitman, 1975.

McConkey, Dale D. *How to Manage by Results*. 3rd ed. New York: American Management Assn., 1976.

3
Line-Item Budgeting

The Foundation of Fiscal Plans

The line-item budget is the most commonly used, probably because of its long history and the ease with which one year's expenses can be compared with the next.

There has been a long tradition of incrementalism in both budgeting and decision making—small changes, made a bit at a time, over time. This tradition is reflected by line-item budgets, each line of which is increased a little bit each year, with no questions asked about the services those expenditures were expected to provide.

The line-item budget format usually summarizes a four-year period: expenditures of the prior period (usually 2 years), with estimates for the current year and the request for the next year. (Figure 15 is a basic line-item budget sheet.) This four-year summary makes it easy to compare amounts of money from one year to the next. Large differences are usually questioned by the finance committee and small, incremental increases are generally unchallenged.

Line-item budgets are normally divided into a few universally used general accounts, which are subdivided according to the specific needs of the organization. Its usefulness as a summary is one reason the line-item format is used to summarize the costs of each program in a budget.

The budget is separated into two areas: operating expenses and capital outlay. Incurred in the course of ordinary activities of the library, operating expenses include personal services, materials and supplies, and contractual services. These items receive annual appropriations, expended annually. In a cash budgeting system, neither expenses nor appropriations can be carried over from one year to

Account Number	Account Title	Actual Expenditures, FY '80	Actual Expenditures, FY '81	Appropriation, FY '82	Actual Expenditures through Dec. '82	Estimated Expenditures, FY '82	Requested for FY '83
100	Personal services						
200	Employee benefits						
300	Materials & supplies						
400	Contractual services						
500	Purchased/lease equipment						
600	Capital outlay						
	Total						

Figure 15. Basic Line-Item Budget Sheet

the next. Capital outlay, on the other hand, is often budgeted over years and both expenses and appropriations can be carried forward.

Following are the fund accounts most commonly used in line-item budgets.

PERSONAL SERVICES

Salaries may be considered one by one or grouped by type of employee: librarian, technical, clerical, and custodial. You identify each person, his or her job title, budgeted salary for the prior period, salary actually paid to date (usually through the first quarter of the current fiscal year), and next year's requested salary.

It won't be unusual for your personnel costs to be greater than 50 percent of your budget.[1] A survey of public libraries for fiscal year 1978 revealed that "staff accounted for the largest expenditure for all public libraries."[2] A survey of public school libraries in 1978 showed that salaries and wages accounted for more than 70 percent of all expenditures.[3]

Salary increases are not discretionary. They are usually derived from a wage scale prepared by the parent organization, negotiated with a union, or determined by the parent organization as a specific percentage increase.

EMPLOYEE BENEFITS

Employers pay part or all of their workers' benefits such as insurance, retirement, and social security. If benefits are paid from the general fund, you may not have to budget for them; otherwise you have to account for them in your budget. There may be one line for benefits, or the account may be divided by benefit type: insurance, retirement, FICA. Retirement and FICA are usually percentages, applied to the employee's salary; insurance costs vary with the individual's coverage.

MATERIALS AND SUPPLIES

Here you budget for all custodial, electrical, plumbing, and office supplies, as well as book, serial, and audiovisual purchases. This will probably be the second largest amount of money budgeted, and may represent about 15 percent of a public library's appropriation.[4]

1. Helen M. Eckard, "NCES Survey of Public Libraries, 1977–78," in *Bowker Annual*, 27th ed. (New York: Bowker, 1982), p.332.

2. Ibid., p.329.

3. Milbrey L. Jones, "NCES Survey of Public School Library Media Centers, 1978," in *Bowker Annual*, 27th ed. (New York: Bowker, 1982), p.341.

4. Eckard, pp.334–335.

CONTRACTUAL SERVICES

Rent and maintenance contracts on buildings and equipment, and service contracts on such things as cataloging, binding, or consulting are contractual or purchased services (sometimes called *purchased services*).

LEASE/PURCHASE EQUIPMENT

Not to be confused with contractual services, this line-item includes only equipment leased for purchase at a later date.

CAPITAL OUTLAY

This outlay represents expenditures for the acquisition of long-term assets such as audiovisual apparatus, remodeling or improvements, equipment, furniture, new construction, and automotive vehicles.

CATEGORICAL FUNDS

Included in this fund are monies with designated uses, such as federal and state grants.

Refining Budget Accounts

You're not stuck with budget accounts just because they've been used in the past. Your common sense will reveal needs to benefit your organization. For example, only the library hires pages. Account 150, which deals with pages, was developed specifically for use by a library.

Think about the regular reports you'll have to prepare for the state library, the school district, or other funding agencies. By planning ahead, you may be able to design your budget format to ease completion of these reports.

Definitions of what may and may not be charged to each line item differ from one organization to another. You may find it difficult to decide whether a purchase is considered equipment or supply. In general, supplies are consumable; they may have to be replaced or replenished within a specified time. Equipment is long lasting. Some parent organizations base the difference on cost alone: anything under a specified amount may be a supply; over that amount, equipment. You must know your organization's definitions and how to apply them as you create and expend your budget.

Discuss the use and definition of accounts with the chief accountant of your parent organization or with your state library consultant. Do this before the beginning of a budget year so you can account for expenditures as they occur.

Focus on Resources, Not Results

Line-item budgets focus on resources. While an expense is assigned to each account, there is no identifiable relationship between money and achievements. For instance, there is no way to tell whether the amount to be spent for personnel equals the results achieved through their efforts. Neither is the focus of their activities identified in this type of budget.

Line-item budgets are, however, somewhat flexible. For example, the general account called Personal Services may be assigned the account number 100. The specific types of employees may be divided as follows: librarians, account 110; technical, 120; clerical, 130; and custodial, 140. You usually have some flexibility among the 100-level accounts. If you overspend in 120 and underspend in 130, it will probably be unchallenged as long as the money allocated for the entire Personal Services account is neither over- nor underspent. But you would have to return to your funding board to get permission to pay unexpectedly high utility bills (account 415) from the unexpended account 300.

There are two premises on which line-item budgeting proceeds: base and fair share. "The base is the general expectation among the participants that programs will be carried on at close to the going level of expenditures."[5] Once a program or an item is budgeted, you can expect that it is accepted and won't be questioned again.

Fair share refers to the expectation that the library's budget will get roughly the same proportion of funds (above or below its established base) as is received by all other city or school departments. Each line item is expected, in turn, to receive its fair-share proportion of funds also.

Line-item budgets lend themselves to incremental increase, and you can use the concept of incrementalism to your advantage in a number of ways. For example, funding board members find it easy to analyze line-item budgets by noticing increases or decreases in accounts from year to year. You can benefit from their analysis by identifying growth or establishing need—whichever is more persuasive.

5. Aaron Wildavsky, *The Politics of the Budgetary Process*, 2nd ed. (Boston: Little, 1974), p.17.

Items that lack public support or understanding may be approved for funding by being placed in large categories so they can't be singled out. For example, your use data may show increasing interest in tape cassettes and a corresponding decline in use of print materials by students, but you know your voting population will disapprove of your emphasis on cassettes. Therefore, you may wish to lump all audiovisual purchases with print materials, into a general line item "Library Materials."

The line-item budget, so widely used, is the foundation for other types of budgets. Therefore, acquaint yourself thoroughly with its advantages and disadvantages. By using it well, you will enhance your image and your effectiveness as a fiscal manager.

The following chapters, on expenditure and revenue projection, detail the development of a line-item budget.

PRACTICE EXPERIENCES

1. Develop a detailed list of the categories on your line-item budget during the last three years. Include special accounts and changes made from year to year. Revise the list by developing what you consider the most effective set of ideal categories. Compare this list with your current year's budget. Discuss differences with a fiscal administrator to clarify their usefulness.

2. From the budget sheets in chapter 4 (figure 16), identify line items which may well be considered library specific.

3. Binding is a contractual service on the sample budget sheets. You may want to include binding costs with your library materials. Assuming the following costs and budget guidelines, which is more advantageous to you?

Current-Year Costs		Budget Increases	
Binding	$ 500	Materials and Supplies	5%
Print Materials	$30,000	Print Materials	20%
		Salaries	7%
		Contractual Services	3%

If you keep binding in 415, how much money will you end up with?

If you move binding to 310, how much money can you expect?

If you account for binding in the 310 account, will you be required to use the extra amount for binding?

SELECTED READINGS

Sweeny, H. W., and Robert Rachlin. *Handbook of Budgeting: Systems and Controls for Financial Management.* New York: Ronald, 1981.

Wildavsky, Aaron. *Budgeting: A Comparative Theory of Budgetary Processes.* Boston: Little, 1975.

———. *The Politics of the Budgetary Process.* 3rd ed. Boston: Little, 1979.

4
Revenue Projections

How Do I Get My Fair Share?

"How can I possibly make a realistic budget request when I don't have any idea how much money they'll give me?" asked one library director. The others in the room nodded their heads in sympathy. "I know I need to start planning earlier," he added, "but I can't wangle any information out of anyone until it's too late. And then I have to hurry."

A library's building, staffing level, and services depend on money and timely information. Whereas your goals may be expansive in fat times and moderate in lean times, they must be regressive in tight-money situations. Although it never hurts to dream about the possibilities inherent in libraries, your time and energy will be best spent if you're realistic about the services *possible* money can buy. A realistic assessment of revenues is a practical starting point for planning expenditures.

This chapter answers various questions you might ask about revenue projection.

> What methods can I use to project revenues?
> What limits should I use in predicting increases or decreases in available funds?
> How can I give my staff appropriate guidelines?
> How can I identify and use an informal communication network?
> What happens if revenue projections are wrong?
> Is it possible to transfer funds from one line item to another?
> Should I count on endowment funds?

These are not easy questions to answer, and the answers may not be the same from year to year. In this chapter you will learn practical ways to reduce some of the unknowns in the revenue projection process.

Budget guidelines, which are provided formally by the parent organization, usually include such items as percentage adjustments for salaries; adjustments in employee benefits due to changes in retirement costs, insurance, and the like; travel restrictions or increases; or adjustments allowable for utilities. These are usually provided for all units of the parent organization and form some of the formal limits on the development of your revenue projections. Typically, such guidelines are stated in terms of percentage increases or decreases, to be computed in revenue projections by each unit (including the library).

Decrease Frustration by Recognizing Reality

It is less frustrating to plan the services of your library and the expenditure of your budget after you have projected revenues. If, for example, you know that you will be allowed no additional staff, supplies will be increased by no more than 2 percent, and your acquisitions budget will be increased by 20 percent, your thinking may go along these lines.

> Twenty percent increase in the acquisitions budget will allow me to purchase an average of x more titles next year.
> Can my technical services staff process those extra titles in a timely manner? Our goal of titles processed per week may have to be changed.
> Will we be able to absorb the extra cost involved in catalog cards, OCLC terminal time, binding supplies, book pockets and book cards?
> Will the circulation staff be able to shelve the new materials? Will there be space? We might have to weed the collection to free up space.

The answers to these questions may lead you to think about the types of materials on which you'll spend the money.

> If we buy reference materials, periodicals, or science books, we'll buy fewer titles for the money and won't need to weed the collection. We also won't need more supplies or staff time.

If we do that, we've made a commitment to continue subscriptions to keep the collection current.

It might be better to spend the 20 percent on more expensive
items, like computer software.

Compare the plans you just made to expend a 20 percent increase
to those you would make if you face no more than a 3 percent increase
in the acquisitions budget.

The purchasing power will be less than this year; so we'll be
buying fewer titles.

This will free technical services staff time and some library
supply money.

I may want to send the staff to computer literacy class so they
can teach our patrons to use the new coin-op computer.

Maybe I should approach the Friends of the Library for computer software. In fact, I think I'd better take a good look
at the library's endowment funds to see if they can be used
for software.

As you can see, varying revenue projections can send you in quite
different planning directions. It is imperative that you learn, as early
as possible, what funding level you can expect.

Whom to Talk To

Budget decision makers begin predicting the availability of future
funds before the current budget has been placed in operation. They
study economic, demographic, and funding trends, as well as expected demands from their organizational units.

Part of your success lies in your ability to analyze the "who" and
the "how" in your parent organization and in the governmental unit
with which appropriations are negotiated. You need to find out how
their predictions will affect you.

Some people throw up their hands in despair when faced with this
question, since they can't count on timely information from the formal system. The formal communication system represents that which
can be published through memoranda, house organs, or newspapers.
Since this information cannot be disseminated in written form until
all uncertainties are laid to rest, it is not timely.

For example, no formal announcements can be made about leg-
islative appropriations before the votes are cast. Assume the state
legislature meets in March, and your budget must be presented by

April for review and approval in June. If you were to await word from the formal system, you would have, at the most, one month in which to calculate the services you could give with your projected revenue.

The formal budgeting system can be considered "for the record." It releases budget guidelines for projecting revenues *once* a year; it requests written and oral budget presentations *once* a year; and the decision makers appropriate funds *once* a year. A once-a-year presentation is not enough to convince or educate funding boards on your needs and service capabilities.

This is why the informal communication system is a far more effective route. You need both timely information and frequent access to the decision makers. They must hear about the library, its services and needs, more than once a year. The informal network speculates about revenues, and is open to information from you. You can be planting ideas about your goals and objectives throughout the year.

THE "IN" CROWD

You can identify and tap into the informal network by approaching people who are at your level on the formal organization chart. Is there a budget analyst with whom you might have coffee? Or an administrative assistant who's "in the know"? During casual conversation, get answers to some very important questions:

> What is the decision-making flow within the organization?
> Who makes fiscal predictions and writes budget guidelines?
> Who else is involved in the informal system?
> Who are the power brokers responsible for tradeoffs from line item to line item and/or from one organizational subunit to another?
> What guidelines are being informally discussed? Which ones have changed since last week, or yesterday?
> Who are significant advisors to the decision makers? (These advisors are often part of both the power-broker group and the informal system. Since they are less visible and vulnerable than the formally identified decision makers, they are often more accessible.)
> How are budget requests heard in the organization? (The formal process is one thing, but the informal information and review system augments your effectiveness in obtaining funds for the library. If you can discuss your revenue

needs informally, and early in the year, you'll more likely be heard during the formal process.)

One way to analyze the informal network is to develop an informal organization chart which parallels the formal one. Fill in the blanks and indicate the networks which flow between the formal and informal systems.

Working from the Outside

How will "working from the outside" help you with revenue projections? Most organizations develop budgets and budget guidelines through at least two major interactions. The first is internal and the second is discussions with governmental units from which major funding commitments are obtained. These can be the state or federal government and/or their regulatory agencies. You should fit them into your organization chart too.

Governmental units often place limits (guidelines) on the allocation of revenues for subsequent years very early in the budget cycle (which they do not make public until much later), but you need to know what they are as early as possible. So listen carefully to your contacts.

"It looks like the salary increase for next year won't be over 7 percent."

"Revenues Office is indicating that overall revenues will be down at least 5 percent next year."

"Since energy costs have gone out of sight, any new money will be dedicated to energy costs."

"This'll be a year of retrenchment, for sure. We'll all be tightening our belts."

Such seemingly casual comments should be taken seriously. Develop more than one contact and get in touch with them every two months during the first half of the budget year and at least once a month during the last half.

Working from the Inside

The more obvious interactions in budget revenue projections are within your parent organization. Most money appropriated to the municipality or school is not designated for specific uses. Most of the internal allocation of funds to the library or to line items is discretionary with the local decision makers. They often establish their own priorities, but are careful not to violate those "suggested" by the major governmental sources of funds. This is a phase of revenue planning about which you must be keenly aware.

Through your informal contacts, you may have input into such decisions. However, you must, at the very least, know the guidelines which are significant to the library budget: salaries, energy costs, equipment, personnel increases or decreases, supplies, and acquisitions.

The more often you're in contact with city or school decision makers, the better. Each "informal" visit is an opportunity to present your views of library needs and to negotiate library allocations.

HOW TO PUT IT TOGETHER

What can you do to be ready to build a realistic budget?

> Develop a file of the names of your informants and dates of contacts. This will summarize the progression of issues through the year.
>
> At the same time, keep a file of public statements by the formal leaders, both within your parent organization and in the governmental agencies through which general funding is obtained.
>
> Discuss with your staff the information you get (but not your sources; people may stop talking with you unless they remain anonymous).
>
> Prepare a chart which identifies the times at which decisions appear to have been made during the year. When are salary guidelines agreed upon? When are total percentage increases agreed upon? When are incremental percentages for various line items discussed? This chart will be useful in subsequent years, allowing you to anticipate the focus of discussions and ask questions at appropriate times.
>
> Be prepared for changes, surprises, and shifts in power and decisions. Organizations are dynamic entities, and the paramount issues shift throughout the year. Keeping in touch and expecting change will prepare you to fulfill your responsibilities as a budget maker.

Use the information you get through the informal system and project your revenues early in the budget cycle. Apply the guidelines to your budget categories and see how they "look." When, finally, you receive the formal budget guidelines, your proposed expenditures will be reasonable, having been tuned to the realities of the revenue picture throughout the year.

Endowment Funds

"I've always viewed endowment funds as discretionary, special-use funds, but they're hardly worth going after now," a library director complained. "My funding board is asking me to project the income from our endowment funds, and then they'll subtract that amount from their appropriation."

Endowment funds can be very useful, especially during lean times. Ideally, they will not be reflected in the library's budget. You don't want your appropriation to be made with those funds subtracted; you want them to remain separate and discretionary.

Each endowment may have various requirements. Some allow you to spend principal and interest; others restrict your spending to interest only. Some specify that they be used only to purchase books, or records, or material on a specific subject.

Give some thought to endowments and, through your board and legal counsel, determine the most beneficial way for people to leave money to the library.

> Should money be left to the municipality, or to the school or library board of trustees?
>
> Are you going to plan a recognition program, such as bookplates, plaques, or published lists of donors?
>
> How will you keep track of gifts given in memory of others? How will you answer the stranger who appears ten years from now, asking to see all the purchases bought in her mother's memory?
>
> Will you need a policy that allows you to "weed" outdated purchases? Should potential benefactors be told that this is a possibility?
>
> Do you prefer restricted funds? Restricted funds can be advantageous if, for example, you can spend the money on only one medium (such as live music) or subject (such as target shooting). You may be able to initiate an excellent concert series or build a notable collection which will bring attention to the library.
>
> Do you prefer unrestricted funds? Left to your discretion, these funds can be used to fund experimental programs until the need for the program is firmly established and the parent organization is willing to fund it.

It is worth your while to provide information about endowments to your public, making it easy for them to leave money to the library. If you prepare a brochure explaining the procedure, you can suggest ways in which they can state their intent and be sure that they will benefit your program.

Carefully developed endowments can allow you to provide unusual or special services. They can also be among your most successful public relations efforts.

Miscalculated Revenue Projections

Earlier in this chapter we said that the budgeting process is dynamic. One of the most unsettling surprises could occur after your budget has been reviewed, approved, and appropriated. You might even be halfway through the fiscal year when the governmental unit from which your funds were appropriated learns that it overestimated its projected revenues. If this happens, you may be asked to *return* funds.

Let's hypothesize that you have been asked to return 2 percent of your budget. The first question is whether the required 2 percent is calculated on the appropriated budget with which you began the year or on the as yet unexpended portion. Two percent of $410,482 (figure 16) is $8,210. If you have expended half the budget, you will have to recover $8,210 from the remaining $205,241—or 4 percent of the remaining funds. But if you calculate 2 percent of $205,241, you have to recover $4,105. It is obviously worth your while to argue for the latter calculation.

Once that question is settled, you have to analyze the unexpended portion of your budget and decide which programs or line items to decrease. If you are working with a program budget, you and your staff have already ranked the programs in order of importance. It will be relatively easy to pick one or two of the lowest-ranking programs to delete or cut back. Although reductions in services are undesirable, they can be explained and justified.

A program budget also allows the possibility of identifying a program which is popular with members of the funding board or their families. By ceasing children's story hours or the lunchtime speakers' program, you may persuade them (through "political" pressure) to leave your budget alone and pursue the $4,105 from other agencies.

If you are working with a line-item budget, it is relatively easy to reduce the remaining budget by 2 percent, but you can never be certain how cutting one line item affects services. (Figure 16 will be used as an example throughout this section.)

You might consider decreasing each fund account by 2 percent. After all, an across-the-board decrease is easy to understand and seems fair to everyone, but your lease/purchase equipment costs will not be less than anticipated, and although the largest part of your budget is personal services, you're determined not to lay off staff.

You then look at capital outlay, and here is an obvious $2,063 to return to the municipality or school system. Although you may regret that you hadn't ordered all the equipment and furniture you had been authorized to buy, the library won't close without that equipment. And if you had placed all the orders and couldn't rescind them, you might have had to turn to more drastic alternatives.

You are left with the contractual services and materials and supplies funds. Unless you decrease library hours, your utility bills, leased equipment, service contracts, and building maintenance are unlikely to change—and you've already expended all of your postage money. This leaves printing, microfilming, binding, and training in the contractual services account. The fact is that you can't really anticipate the impact of decreasing those line items.

You finally decide it will be easiest to subtract the remaining $2,042 from the materials and supplies account. You'll buy fewer titles and supplies this year than planned. Because acquisitions represent a large percentage of the budget, and the money represents only 3 percent of the print budget, why not? It doesn't seem to make that much difference, in the short run.

Miscalculations of revenues are out of your control, but they happen; and the control you have over your budget and its support of services are vitally important. You must be sure it has been designed to provide you with the management data you need in all circumstances. Also, you must be able to look at the long-run effects of budget cuts. In the above example, you cannot be sure what the long-run effect will be from cutting the most meaningful service you offer.

Transfers among Funds

Although line-item budgets are less-than-ideal management tools for preparing budget cuts, they are flexible when you must deal with internal fund transfers. The expenditure of each 300-level line item need not balance what was budgeted as long as the *entire* Materials and Supplies account balances.

For example, if you were to buy computer software from your nonprint account (320), you would probably spend more than the appropriated $1,914. That will most likely be unchallenged, as long

Account Number	Account Title	Actual Expenditures, FY '80	Actual Expenditures, FY '81	Appropriation, FY '82	Actual Expenditures through Dec. '82	Estimated Expenditures, FY '82	Requested for FY '83
100	Personal services	259,447	267,231	280,592	140,296	280,592	
300	Materials & supplies	70,611	72,729	76,366	38,396	74,324	
400	Contractual services	45,669	47,034	49,386	25,511	49,386	
500	Lease/purchase	2,000	2,060	2,075	1,038	2,075	
600	Capital outlay	1,826	1,882	2,063	—	0	
Total		379,553	390,936	410,482	205,241	406,377	
100	Personal services	259,447	267,231	280,592	140,296	280,592	
310	Print materials	60,908	62,736	65,875	31,046	63,883	
320	Nonprint	1,770	1,870	1,914	1,800	1,914	
330	Office	3,272	3,375	3,538	1,500	3,488	
335	Custodial	1,947	2,000	2,160	2,000	2,160	
340	Electrical	1,770	1,775	1,914	1,200	1,914	
345	Plumbing	708	730	765	650	765	
350	Safety	236	243	200	200	200	
Total		70,611	72,729	76,366	38,396	74,324	

405	Postage	1,104	1,137	1,472	1,472	1,472
410	Telephone	1,922	1,998	2,078	1,039	2,078
415	Light & heat	25,464	26,209	28,239	14,120	28,239
420	Water	295	303	319	160	319
430	Printing	1,123	1,100	1,012	400	1,012
435	Microfilm	1,121	1,208	1,212	1,000	1,212
440	Binding	826	853	891	290	891
445	Auto. maint.	110	110	120	60	120
450	Leased equip.	564	588	612	306	612
455	Bldg. maint.	12,685	13,060	13,018	6,509	13,018
460	Training	354	364	304	100	304
470	Service contracts	101	104	109	55	109
	Total	45,669	47,034	49,386	25,511	49,386
510	Computer	--	--	--	--	--
520	Copy machine	1,200	1,236	1,296	648	1,296
530	Stationwagon	800	824	779	390	779
	Total	2,000	2,060	2,075	1,038	2,075
610	Furniture	--	800	114	0	0
615	Equipment	1,249	441	1,294	0	0
620	AV equip.	577	641	655	0	0
	Total	1,826	1,882	2,063	0	0

Figure 16. Sample Line-Item Budget (in Dollars)

as the entire Materials and Supplies expenditure balances with its appropriation. It is not as easy to move money from one fund account to another. If you try to buy computer software from your acquisitions budget, your accounting department may return the purchase requisition, thinking software is capital outlay.

To move money from the 320 account to the 615 account, you have to make a special request, justifying the need, at a hearing before the finance board or budget committee. This is not impossible, however; you follow the same thought processes you used when you justified the budget. If you have established your need, considered alternatives and chosen the most sensible one, and can explain it clearly, your request is likely to be honored.

Summary

Revenue projections are made before budget preparation; and it is upon expected money that you determine service levels. But the process doesn't stop there. The revenue picture can change any time during the budget year:

> You may be asked to return an unexpended portion of your appropriation to your funding body.
> You may be "blessed" with a donation (such as a computer) which makes unanticipated demands on other line items.
> Unforeseen price increases could occur during the year for services you are committed to purchase.

These are a few challenges which crop up during the fiscal year. The next chapter continues the process of budget expenditure.

PRACTICE EXPERIENCES

1. Develop an informal organization chart of your parent organization which parallels its formal organization chart.

2. Identify and develop at least two informal communication contacts within the fiscal branch of your parent organization.

3. Establish a file of formal guidelines for revenue projections. If you are in a position to do so, develop a file of informal guidelines also.

4. Develop guidelines for an ideal endowment fund, considering ways of responding to the questions posed in this chapter.

5. Working with the budget in figure 16, identify two more ways to recover $4,105 from the unexpended funds. How could you recover $8,210?

SELECTED READINGS

Dixon, Robert L. *The Executive's Accounting Primer.* 2nd ed. New York: McGraw-Hill, 1982.

Prentice, Ann E. *Public Library Finance.* Chicago: ALA, 1977.

Spiro, Herbert T. *Finance for the Nonfinancial Manager.* 2nd ed. New York: Wiley, 1982.

5
Expenditure Projections

Projecting of expenditures is a major step in the preparation of your budget. Chapters 1, 2, and 3 provided the foundation concepts of budget development, and in chapter 4 you learned about critical issues in projecting revenues. Now you are ready to develop the second part of your budget—the part most people refer to as *the* budget: expenditure projections. This chapter will suggest the most commonly used processes for doing so. However, since it is largely an explanation of the computational processes, you need to keep in mind the previous four chapters and refer to them with regularity.

For instance, the program-budgeting information and ranking in the "Practice Experiences" in chapter 2 will prove invaluable as you compute your budget expenditures in this chapter. The expected levels of revenues, projected through application of chapter 4, provide the foundation for your decisions about your expenditures.

The major objectives in this chapter are

Identification of sources of expenditure-projection information

Description of the significance of expenditure projection in budget development

Computation of the impact of inflation on expenditures

Development of a three-year expenditure analysis chart

Development of a subsequent-year expenditure-projection chart.

How Much Is Enough?

Projecting budget expenditures is a critical and demanding function, which librarians, as managers, are expected to carry out. As you look forward to each budget year, you will consider many uses of your anticipated revenues. Your major challenge is to make accurate and acceptable projections of expenditures for these programs. To overestimate needed funds may seem to be a comfortable approach; however, *overprojecting* has two effects:

> All of the funds might not be used, leaving you vulnerable to *underfunding* the following year.
>
> If the amount of funds for each budget category is inaccurately projected, some categories may not have sufficient funds. Later requests for fund transfers (chapter 4) among categories are often considered poor practice by funding agencies. On the other hand, underestimating may leave you struggling to achieve your objectives for the entire budget year, and vulnerable during the next budget request period. It is therefore extremely important to learn to project budget expenditure fully and accurately.

What Approach?

Two approaches can be utilized to develop accurate budget projections. They involve looking back at actual expenditures and looking ahead to development of an accurate projection.

How can you look back to extract and use appropriate data and information from previous years' budgets? You should obtain copies of the budgets for the two previous years of operation and for the current year. These budgets should be in your files; if not, they can usually be obtained through your accounting or principal's office. (If you are a student, you may be able to get copies of the library budgets through a school bookkeeper, a city accountant, or your state librarian.) To supplement them and to focus your efforts, you might also read the library's annual reports.

The first step in making projections is to get all the information you can about the uses of budgeted money for the past two years and the current year, that is, how all available revenues for that period were budgeted and used. Remember, you need to get both the approved budget and the final budget for each year. The approved budget authorizes expenditures while the final budget shows actual expenditures. These figures are often different (usually due to line-item transfers or to underspending certain accounts); so both are important to you in making projections.

Posting

Once you have the data from the past and the current years in hand, you are ready to *post* the comparative budget items. First, make sure that the layout or format for each of the years is the same. The budget categories should match, whether they are line items or program format. If they do not appear to be the same, ask the accounting office or a librarian for assistance in matching expenditure categories for these years. (Changes in nomenclature, which frequently occur in budget formats, do not necessarily reflect actual changes in budget items.) You need to make these determinations before proceeding. For instance, "Contractual Services" as a line category one year may become "Purchased Services" in a subsequent year's budget.

It will be easier to deal with the overall budget figures by line items at first. Later, you may want to construct a chart for each program of the library, as explained in chapter 2. To post the expenditures, copy figure 17 or develop a similar one of your own. There should be a separate line for each category which has been or will be used in the budgets. Take the approved budget figures for the second year back and place them in the first column on the chart. Place the figures for the next two years in the appropriate columns. Next, take the final or actual budget expenditures for each line-item category and place them in the "final" column for each specific year. This will give you a visual layout of the changes. Next year's projections will be placed on figure 18.

However, before you go on to figure 18 you must analyze the information you have collected. For each budget line item, compute

> The percent change from the first year back to the second year back. Divide column 5 by column 2, then subtract 1. Enter the result into column 3. If the result is less than 1, place it in parentheses.
>
> The percent change from the first year back to the current year. Divide column 8 by column 5, subtract 1, and enter the result in column 6.
>
> The percent change from the second year back to the current year (the total percent change). Divide column 8 by column 2, subtract 1, and enter the result in column 9.

Inflationary Impact

Ascertain the national inflation rate for each year.[1] Any increase beyond the inflation rate is probably due to actual growth or change

1. *Reader's Digest 1983 Almanac and Yearbook* (Pleasantville, N.Y., Reader's Digest Association), pp.196–197.

Program: _____

	1 1981 Approved	2 1981 Final	3 1982–81 Final %	4 1982 Approved	5 1982 Final	6 1983–82 Final %	7 1983 Approved	8 1983 Projected Expd.	9 1983–1981 %
Personal services									
Librarian									
Technical									
Custodial									
Other (specify)									
Benefits									
FICA									
PERA									
Group insurance									
Other (specify)									
Matls. & supplies									
Books									
Periodicals									
AV materials									
Office									
Custodial									
Electrical									
Plumbing									
Safety									

Continued

Figure 17. Projecting Expenditures from Previous Expenditures

	1 1981 Approved	2 1981 Final	3 1982–81 Final %	4 1982 Approved	5 1982 Final	6 1983–82 Final %	7 1983 Approved	8 1983 Projected Expd.	9 1983–1981 %
Contractual service									
Postage	—	—	—	—	—	—	—	—	—
Bldg. maint.	—	—	—	—	—	—	—	—	—
Training	—	—	—	—	—	—	—	—	—
Travel	—	—	—	—	—	—	—	—	—
Postage	—	—	—	—	—	—	—	—	—
Telephone	—	—	—	—	—	—	—	—	—
Light & heat	—	—	—	—	—	—	—	—	—
Water	—	—	—	—	—	—	—	—	—
Printing	—	—	—	—	—	—	—	—	—
Lease/purchase	—	—	—	—	—	—	—	—	—
Capital outlay									
Bldg. improvements	—	—	—	—	—	—	—	—	—
Equipment	—	—	—	—	—	—	—	—	—
Furniture	—	—	—	—	—	—	—	—	—
Other (specify)	—	—	—	—	—	—	—	—	—

Figure 17. Continued

Program: _____

	Most Recent Inflation Factor or Price Index	Factor for New or Additional Services	Next Year's Expenditure Projection
Personal services			
Librarian	_____	_____	_____
Technical	_____	_____	_____
Custodial	_____	_____	_____
Other (specify)	_____	_____	_____
Benefits	_____	_____	_____
FICA	_____	_____	_____
PERA	_____	_____	_____
Group insurance	_____	_____	_____
Other (specify)	_____	_____	_____
Matls. & supplies	_____	_____	_____
Books	_____	_____	_____
Periodicals	_____	_____	_____
AV materials	_____	_____	_____
Office	_____	_____	_____
Custodial	_____	_____	_____
Electrical	_____	_____	_____
Plumbing	_____	_____	_____
Safety	_____	_____	_____
Contractual service	_____	_____	_____
Postage	_____	_____	_____
Bldg. maint.	_____	_____	_____
Training	_____	_____	_____
Travel	_____	_____	_____
Postage	_____	_____	_____
Telephone	_____	_____	_____
Light & heat	_____	_____	_____
Water	_____	_____	_____
Printing	_____	_____	_____
Lease/purchase	_____	_____	_____
Capital outlay	_____	_____	_____
Bldg. improvements	_____	_____	_____
Equipment	_____	_____	_____
Furniture	_____	_____	_____
Other (specify)	_____	_____	_____

Figure 18. Projecting Expenditures for Changing Services

in library programs. However, exceptions will exist. In recent years, prices of materials and utilities have grown more quickly than the consumer price index. Your annual reports should assist you in identifying the reasons for this growth (or decrease). Make notes on these changes so you will have them readily available as you continue your analysis.

Questions to be asked are

Are these programs going to continue to increase (or decrease) for the next year? If so, at the rate indicated from year to year on your chart? Not as much? More? Try to be as realistic as possible. If a program or area of service is declining, project the decrease (unless you have a valid reason not to do so).

Are there programs or activities which will demand increases in line items to provide adequate support?

Are major changes in personnel anticipated which will affect the line-item trends? For example, retirements result in replacement of personnel by less experienced and, therefore, less expensive persons.

Have there been major shifts in demand on library services which may result in greater (or lesser) fund demands in any of the line items?

As these kinds of questions are posed and answered for each program and each line item, the basis for projecting to the next year's budget expenditure is clarified. Figure 18 will help to organize this information for line items. The information gathered in preparing figure 18 and the notes you have taken are essential in making your projections.

Increases are based on increased demand for services and on the projected impact of inflation on each line item. The impact of inflation may vary from one line item to another. Book prices, for instance, probably will increase at a greater rate than salaries or supplies. Sources of information, like the *Bowker Annual*, may help you establish such projections. Utilities may increase at a greater rate than books. (Your parent organization usually has a *factor* for you to use for utility increases.) As the cost of utilities is projected for each separate library, the resulting information may influence your decisions. For instance, if small branch libraries or school libraries are comparatively expensive to operate, this information may be a basis for closing them or radically altering their hours of operations.

Impact of Programs and Services

After you have dealt with inflationary increases, increases in programs and services must be considered. It is at this point that your established goals become vitally important. As you completed your needs assessment in chapter 1 and identified your programs in chapter 2, you identified these goals. Now, as you begin to project expenditures, your major concern is to provide the necessary support to accomplish those goals.

Of course, if the projection of expenditures exceeds the projection of revenues, only two possibilities exist:

> Increase proposed revenues.
> Reduce proposed expenditures.

The goals to be accomplished and the programs to be offered would be reduced by the latter action. As you may have observed, program budgeting provides an excellent basis for such decisions. Your resulting budget should provide an alignment of goals and expenditures to achieve your goals for the subsequent year.

Expenditure Analysis Chart

Completion of figures 17 and 18 is necessary before you proceed with the expenditure-projection process. For example, let's look at a line item for audiovisual materials (figure 19).

Your needs assessment may have identified a major increase in use of AV materials due to the shift from print materials to increasingly available media-based materials. You proceed by computing the percentage of difference from the various years. The second year back to the first year back is an increase of $180 (or 8.1%) in the approved budget and an increase of $252 (or 11.7%) in the final expenditures.

Materials	1 1981 Approved	2 1981 Final	3 1982–81 Final %	4 1982 Approved	5 1982 Final	6 1983–82 Final %	7 1983 Approved	8 1983 Projected Expd.	9 1983–81 Total % Change
Books									
Periodicals/ newspapers									
AV	$2,220	$2,144	11.7	$2,400	$2,396	50.2	$3,600	$3,600	67.9

Figure 19. Sample Expenditure Projection: Materials Budget

The first year back to the current year is an increase of $1,200 (or 50%) in the approved budget and an increase of $1,204 (or 50.2%) from final to projected expenditures. The second year back to the current year is an increase of $1,380 (or 62%) for the approved budget and $1,456 (or 67.9%) from the final to projected expenditures.

Differences between approved budget increases and final budget increases are not critical, unless they are extreme. Extreme increases or decreases need to be taken into account and explained as they relate to projections for the subsequent year. These figures are entered in the appropriate columns in figure 17.

In figure 18, for instance, you may have identified (through your suppliers) an estimated inflation factor of 18 percent for AV materials for next year. You also have identified that you would like to increase your services in this area by approximately 15 percent through the provision of new materials. Therefore, you can project in two ways:

> Divide your column-9 increase by 2 ($\div$ 2), resulting in an overall per year increase of approximately 34 percent, to which you add the 18 percent inflation factor, for a 52 percent total increase.
> Or use the estimates of 15 percent for services increase and add the 18 percent inflation factor, for a 33 percent increase.

The results of the first method would be $5,472, and the second method would yield $4,788. Your decision as to which method to use would be based on your assessment of the possibilities of substantiating your request at your budget hearings.

Other Resources

To obtain the information to assist you in making these projections, a number of additional sources can be identified and used. The experiences and observations of your staff should be invaluable in making projections. The interaction of the staff may also result in creative approaches to managing expenditures and facilitating goal accomplishment. Suppliers, jobbers, and vendors can be contacted for prices or for estimates of inflationary impact on their products or services. They usually know what the price increase will be in their businesses well in advance of your operational year. You should contact them and obtain this information.

The *Bowker Annual* and articles on U.S. periodical and serial services price indexes, which appear in *Library Journal,* are excellent sources of information for historical price-increase trends. The price/cost indexing system for books and serials which they provide will permit you to justify larger-than-inflation increases in your budget. These sources offer a more reliable cost-projection system for books and serials than using the standard rate of inflation, since they relate specifically to books and serials (rather than *all* goods and services).

For instance, a review of price changes from 1982 to 1983 reveals that periodicals in chemistry and physics increased 16.9 percent, in journalism and communications 10.3 percent, in labor and industrial relations 18.2 percent, and in library and information science 9.5 percent.[2] Increases in excess of the standard rate of inflation should be used in interpreting your budget increases to decision makers in your parent organization.

Changes in Emphasis

Decisions about developing the collection are ongoing, but your emphasis may be different from year to year, and this may affect your projected book and serial expenditures. For example, one of your new programs may be to further support the business community by building the business collection. Or the school may be beginning a fine arts program and you are expected to develop an art collection which would support it. The *Bowker Annual* presents a chart of average per volume prices of hardcover books from year to year. It lists subject categories with Dewey Decimal Classification numbers.

In 1981, the average price of a business book was $21.02 and the average price of an art book $32.18. The amounts are meaningful when compared with fiction, which averaged $13.38 per volume.[3] Therefore, using this example, you might prefer to deemphasize one area of the collection to buy business books from the current year's budget. Buying art materials would certainly require that you project a sizable expenditure for the subsequent year's book budget.

What Percent for Books, What for Serials?

If books and serials are on the same line of the budget, you will have to make a conscious decision about the percentage you are willing

2. Norman B. Brown and Jane Phillips, "Price Indexes for 1983: U.S. Periodicals and Serial Services," *Library Journal* (Sept. 1, 1983), p.1659.

3. Chandler B. Grannis, "Book Title Output and Average Prices, 1981 Preliminary Figures," *Bowker Annual,* 27th ed. (New York: Bowker, 1982), p.388.

to spend on each. There was a 250.7 percent increase in the price of serials from 1967 to 1979,[4] requiring a cutback in serial purchases or a decision to spend ever larger percentages of materials money on periodicals. The need to maintain expensive serial titles may not be as strong in the public library as it is in a school, where journal subscriptions are necessary support for curricula. A yearly analysis of the balance between serials and monographs should be a routine part of the projection of expenditures. You, as a manager, can make a reasoned projection which can be included in your budget presentation.

Summary

You must get your city's or institution's guidelines for inflation and acceptable levels of budget increases. In a few areas, such as salaries and benefits, these must be used for projections. In other areas the guidelines are somewhat flexible and are provided to assist you in considering budget changes. When you exceed the guidelines in the flexible areas, you must be prepared to provide descriptions, explanations, and data to assist budget decision makers in understanding the basis for your expenditure projections.

As you work with the projection for each line item, bring all your data together and establish your rationale for the proposed expenditures. This rationale will be the basis for your budget presentation to your library board, your council, or your chief administrator.

PRACTICE EXPERIENCES

1. Complete figure 17 for your library. Complete figure 18 for your next year's budget.
2. Rate yourself on your completion of figures 17 and 18 on a scale of 1 to 9: 9 = highest rating (you completed all sections); 6 = middle rating (you completed about 2/3 of the chart); 3 = low rating (you completed about 1/3 of the chart).

---

4. Michael R. Kronenfeld and James A. Thompson, "The Impact of Inflation on Journal Costs," *Library Journal* (Apr. 1, 1981), p.714.

SELECTED READINGS

Brown, Norman B., and Jane Phillips. "Price Indexes for 1982: U.S. Periodicals and Serial Services." *Library Journal*, pp.1379–1382 (Aug. 1982).

Dessauer, John P. "Book Industry Markets, 1976–1985." *Book Industry Trends, 1981*, Research Report No. 11. New York: Book Industry Study Group, 1981.

Goldhor, Herbert. "U.S. Public Library Statistics in Series: A Bibliography and Subject Index." *Bowker Annual*, 28th ed., pp.327–336. New York: Bowker, 1983.

Grannis, Chandler B. "Book Title Output and Average Prices, 1982 Preliminary Figures." *Bowker Annual of Library and Book Trade Information*, 28th ed., pp.371–379. New York: Bowker, 1983.

Piper, Nelson A. "Prices of U.S. and Foreign Published Materials." *Bowker Annual*, 28th ed., pp.385–403. New York: Bowker, 1983.

6
Exceptional Sources of Revenue

Why Consider Other Revenue Sources?

Not all the projects undertaken by your library will be funded.
Through your needs assessment planning activities, you will almost
certainly come up with more needs than money (chapter 1). Additionally, when the program budgets are planned and ranked, some
are excluded from funding (chapter 2). As the budget year proceeds,
you may become aware of new needs for which there are no resources, unless you were to reallocate funds. Reallocation might be
neither politically wise, in view of your relationship to your funding
agency, nor economically possible, if you are to fulfill the goals and
objectives for which you planned.

You are caught in a dilemma: to postpone responding to the new
needs until the next budget year or to pursue other alternatives. This
chapter includes ideas which might help you meet this new challenge
by suggesting *exceptional sources of revenues*—that is, funds for the exceptions which arise outside your planned operation or which were
not funded by appropriated revenues. The chapter will suggest resources useful in locating such funds and ideas about some of the
critical questions to be answered in pursuit of such funds.

Getting the Money

Following are two conversations, representing different approaches
to funding sources. In one library, you might hear this conversation:

> "I hear they're funding programs for the handicapped this year. Let's get the money for a TTY or some large-print books. That way we'll have more acquisition money for other things."

> "That may be a good idea. How many visually impaired people are there in this city?"

> "I don't know, but who cares? That's where the money is this year. Let's get our share."

A different discussion may be pursued in another library:

> "Some of our elderly patrons have been complaining about the large-print books we bought last year. They're too heavy to hold. What do you think we should do?"

> "I understand there are funds available for that sort of thing. Let's look into some of the other large-print publishers and see if we can find something lighter in weight. While we're at it, let's survey our patrons to see if they'd be interested in large-print crossword puzzles.

> "In fact, let's see if we can get another library to work with us. We could share resources that way—we can get twice as many titles at half the cost."

> "That's a terrific idea. In fact, the LSCA guidelines *recommend* funding for cooperative projects. We can't go wrong."

These are two approaches to seeking exceptional sources of funding. You can identify the kinds of projects which are in vogue at the moment and create a "need" to meet the funding requirements, or you can define your program needs and then seek funding.

Before Writing a Proposal

The need is identified as a part of your regular needs assessment procedure (chapter 1). The special need for which you might seek funding may represent a new area of activity for the library, or it may be low on your priority list. New areas of activity are often difficult to introduce into a lean budget or at a time in which budget reductions are the reality. Low priorities are often areas of need that simply cannot be funded due to the ranking process. Sometimes, however, these needs coincide with special funding interests of the federal or state government.

Occasionally, inquiries from special groups or institutions within your community will call your attention to revenue resources. Or you may become aware of funds through your research into possible sources of grant money. However you become aware of them, you will carefully consider the time involved in both proposal preparation and fund administration. Grant administration often requires more oversight and evaluation than you may wish to spend. But even when these requirements are considered, it may seem to be worthwhile.

Is It Fundable?

Once you identify a program idea or isolate a need, you have to determine whether it is fundable from an exceptional source of revenue. Therefore, study of various reference sources should be a basic part of every librarian's education. (A number of reference sources are described later in this chapter.) It takes hard work to become familiar with sources, but the effort is worthwhile if you develop a grant proposal. Once you are familiar with the references and the possibilities they suggest for funding, the next time a program need is identified (which cannot be covered with local funding) you will have a good idea whether it might be fundable from a special source and you will know whether to proceed with planning and application.

Except for locating sources of funds and tailoring your proposal to their special requirements, the grant-getting process is a miniature exercise in program budgeting, such as you studied in chapter 2.

Steps in the Process

First, assess the impact of the grant on your institution: its potential positive and negative effects within the organization. For instance, will the library staff be able to process the number of volumes you plan to buy with the money you are seeking? Will your acquisitions budget be cut by the administration because you received a grant, thereby decreasing your appropriated base of funds—and decreasing the impact of future percentage increases from regular budget sources? If you apply for a grant to allow you the experience of working in another library for six months, will the current staffing level be adequate for the necessary library activities? If so, how will you justify your position, if you can be away six months and there is no negative effect on your library's operation? How will you arrange coverage while you are gone?

Questions of this nature must be asked as part of your initial assessment of the impact of a grant on your institution, before you get into the details of writing the grant proposal. Your assessment of the effects of grant money on the institution should address the impact on staff, services, processes, and regular funding.

Second, perform a needs assessment to be sure that the need you perceive exists and is high among the priorities of the library staff, board, and community (see chapter 1).

Third, search the literature to discover whether your idea has been tried before and with what results. For instance, has a "packaged" program for children already been accomplished elsewhere? Has a collection of suitable books for elderly citizens been identified? Do materials exist which describe the significant subcultures in your area? Have other states already developed a shared information base system for archives?

Such programs have been funded through exceptional sources of revenues for various libraries across the nation during recent years. When you write your proposal, you will want to cite such activities to obtain credibility for your ideas.

Fourth, make sure that the support from your community is identified and included in the proposal. Support may be confirmed by any "hard" or "soft" match of funds required by the grant. However, letters of support are also useful.

Fifth, investigate the various funding sources, select one, and through a telephone inquiry confirm that your idea will interest that source. Then follow the telephone conversation with a letter. When you receive the application form and instructions, write the proposal, directing it at the requirements and expectations of that funding source.

The format of proposals varies among funding sources, but the general-information requirement is usually similar.[1] Three issues are critical to funding sources:

> Importance of the problem
> Value of the solution
> Demonstrated ability to carry out the project.

Ask for Help

At this point you need to contact the administration, or the city or town accountant. There may be matching funds or in-kind contributions the library, school, or city will be required to make.

1. Howard Hillman and Marjorie Chamberlain, *The Art of Winning Corporate Grants* (New York: Vanguard, 1980).

Do not be discouraged if a granting agency requires a *hard* or *soft* match. A hard match refers to an equal-dollar amount which is a stipulation of the grant. This is often more difficult to get than a soft match (or in-kind contribution) because it involves the commitment of real money.

It is important to discuss hard-match requirements with your accountant or fiscal manager to determine if hard-match monies are available and whether you can submit such a proposal. Generally, an official statement of hard-match availability is needed when the proposal packet is sent to the funding agency.

A soft match is the most common matching requirement. The amount will differ among granting agencies, and "creativity" in defining such contributions is needed on your part. Soft-match ideas include:

> If equipment owned by the library will be used during the project, you can assign a rental fee to it and make this dollar amount your donation to the project.
>
> If you rely on staff to carry out the project, you can declare an appropriate percentage of their salaries in-kind contributions. (This can be applied under some definitions of hard match as well.)
>
> If meetings of an unpaid advisory board are part of your program, the cost of their transportation to those meetings can be declared part of your match.

Your fiscal officers (having prepared grant proposals before) will be able to make many suggestions about meeting the required grant obligations.

Proposal Writing

Proposals are like the written budget presentation you make to your board every year. Begin with a description of your library: its location, staff and collection size, and clientele. (This "sets the scene" for what follows and suggests that you and your institution are credible. The description could be patterned after that of Midtown library in chapter 2.)

Then present a problem statement which is substantiated by your needs assessment. Be sure to use appropriate statistics—objective facts—and be client centered.

Let's pick a problem from the Midtown example: "The elderly population is increasing due to the development of a major retirement village in the old south-side community." The formulation of the problem could read:

A recent study of population changes in Midtown (conducted with Midtown's continuing urban renewal planning) has identified a 20 percent increase in residents over 60 years of age in the 50-square-block area of the city known as South Side. A major part of this increase has been due to the opening of a "retirement village" in that area. The library has contact with this village and, as a result, has developed a collection of large-print books. However, according to a survey conducted among 100 patrons who use the collection, over 50 percent of the books are too heavy for them to handle comfortably. Additionally, over 60 percent of the residents of the village do not have transportation to the main library, where the collection is housed. There is no branch library.

Set forth your objectives, which should be attainable, measurable, timely, and client centered. Follow with your methods or procedures and a justification for choosing these particular plans and resources. The objectives of your project are

An agreement with the retirement village for expanded library services at the village center
A survey to determine the reading interests of the population
An additional 100 titles of large-print books for the special collection. These books will represent the interests of readers identified in the survey and will be of a size and weight for easy handling
To subscribe to at least 20 periodicals which are identified as of interest to the readers
A circulation center, in operation in the retirement village not later than December 1
To hire residents of the village as part-time circulation staff.

Then, in justification of the project, write something like this:

It is the intent of this project to provide the greatest possible service to the elderly citizens by meeting their identified needs directly. It appears to us that establishing a small collection and circulation center provides a simple answer.

One of our intentions, should this proposal be funded, is to hire part-time assistants from the village to staff the circulation center. Funds are requested for this purpose. Hiring part-time assistants will be less expensive than providing regular library staff. Basic supervision and assistance will be provided through the regular library staff as part of the required match.

Next, identify a "time frame" in which the need will be met, the staff provided (as well as the fiscal agent you will use), and how the results of the program will be disseminated (see figure 20). A Gantt chart (such as this) can identify your methods and procedures clearly and easily. If needed, a description of each item on the chart could be provided in narrative form. (This decision is determined by the instructions in the proposal guide you have acquired from the funding agency.)

The time lines are identified in figure 20. However, it should be noted in the proposal that if the December opening is to be met, a funding decision is needed not later than June 1. If the decision is later, the opening will be correspondingly later.

The results of this outreach activity will be disseminated through a project report, provided to your agency six months after establishment of the circulation center. The report will include acquisitions problems and issues, selection of books and periodicals, circulation information, staffing experiences, and other information which would be useful.

A vital part of your proposal is evaluation of the program—both the end product (*product* evaluation) and the methods used to attain it (*process* evaluation). Process evaluation includes procedures which monitor the implementation of a project, such as

Time lines: Are things being done when they were projected?

	Apr.	May	June	July	Aug.	Sept.	Oct.	Nov.	Dec.
Agreement	---								
Survey		---							
Book acquisition			---	---	---	---	---		
Periodical subscription			---						
Cataloging						---	---	---	---
Center plans			---	---	---	---	---	---	
Staffing						---	---	---	---
Set up								---	---
Opening of center									---

Figure 20. Gantt Chart for Grant Application

Data gathering: Are data identified? Are formal procedures initiated so that the data needed at the end of the project will have been gathered?

Procedures: Are procedures developed and carried out which might be expected to lead the project to a successful conclusion?

People issues: Have the appropriate people been involved, hired, and oriented so that the project is facilitated through their efforts?

Fiscal control: Have fiscal control policies and procedures been developed and are they used?

Remember, the focus of this phase of evaluation is monitoring the process as it takes place.

Product evaluation, the other phase, deals with formal questions (which must be answered) about the overall effectiveness and efficiency of the project.

Were the purposes (goals and objectives) for which the project was initiated achieved?

Does the public feel the project was worthwhile?

What conclusions do the summary data support?

What has been (should be) done to assure the continuance of services, materials, etc., after the end of the project?

What were the impacts of the project on the organization and on its ability to carry out its mission?

Plan the evaluation process as an integral and ongoing part of the program and plan to gather your data for the final evaluation as part of the process of project management. Only in this way can you demonstrate the results of implementation of the proposal.

Again, evaluation will be carried out in two phases: process and product. The process evaluation includes information and answers to the following issues:

1. The working agreement was established with the retirement village. (A copy will be attached as a model for other programs.) Completion date will be no later than April 30.

2. The survey was conducted within the time frame and had at least 60 percent participation by residents. Completion date will be no later than May 31.

3. At least 100 additional titles of large-print books, of appropriate size and weight, were identified and ordered no

later than June 30 and received no later than September 30.

4. At least 20 periodicals were identified and ordered no later than June 30 and received no later than November 1.
5. Acquired materials were cataloged no later than November 15.
6. Plans for the circulation center were developed and approved no later than September 30.
7. An initial group of part-time staff, selected from among residents of the center, were hired and oriented no later than December 1.
8. An appropriate opening ceremony was planned, to be carried out no later than December 1.

The product evaluation is organized to provide information and answers to the following:

1. How the objectives of the project were met. Variance will be explained and information provided to assess the success of the project.
2. Circulation rate of books and periodicals during the first six months of the project. Also, the number of participants and their satisfaction with the program will be described. Recommendations will be made (as suggested by this information) to improve circulation participation.
3. Descriptive information will explain the staffing and its effectiveness. Analyses of patterns of staffing, staffing problems, and issues will be carried out. Recommendations for improvement will be made.
4. Additions and expansions to the program will be provided, with funding approaches to support them.
5. Funding to sustain the circulation center, after the period supported through the project, will be described. This will assure the funding agency that efforts will be continued if it is determined that the project is successful in terms of items 1, 2, and 3 of this product evaluation.

Address the need for future funding as well. Funding sources are always interested in what it will take to maintain the program after they have supplied start-up funds and where you plan to get future support. The best plans for future support are those which do not require continuing outside funding (i.e., those which become self-supporting).

Prepare a budget. It should be realistic, accurate, and justifiable. Do not underestimate the cost, thinking you will be more likely to get funding if the budget is small. The budget you prepare should match the objectives and should be easily audited. If there is a need for matching, your budget should be presented in two columns (see figure 21). The matching percentage should represent the amount required by the funding source.

In addition to various ways of identifying matches, your fiscal officers will tell you what indirect or overhead cost to state in your budget. A percentage of your request (established by the institution or city), it reflects the cost of administering a grant. (Examples are light, heat, space, bookkeeping, and payroll costs.) This percentage is added to your budget request, and is occasionally negotiable with the grant-making agency. Whether negotiable or not, it will increase the amount of the request; therefore, it will increase the amount of the required match.

After this work is finished, write a one-page abstract of the who, why, what, when, where, and cost questions.

Prepare the appendixes, which will include letters of support, statistics, and resumés of the principal investigator and staff.

Review the entire proposal with your staff, your board, and your school or town/city administration.

Item	Funds Requested	Local Match
Salaries	——	——
Fringe benefits	——	——
Consultants and contract services, e.g., bookkeeping, auditing, public relations	——	——
Space costs	——	——
Rental, lease, and purchase of equipment	——	——
Consumable supplies	——	——
Travel	——	——
Telephone	——	——
Other (identify)	——	——
Indirect costs @ _____ % (as required by local support agency)	——	——

Figure 21. Budget for Grant Application

Submit the application—and wait for the money to come. If you are not successful the first time around, don't let your work go to waste. Submit the proposal to another source of funding, or make the changes suggested by the first funding source. In either case, you may have to emphasize a different angle or approach to meet the agency's criteria, with the same tenacity you show every year at your budget presentation.

Where to Find Information

While cuts in library budgets are publicized, we also see that other-than-tax-dollar sources of revenue are tapped by libraries. LSCA, NEH, ECIA, and HEA are familiar acronyms for federal granting agencies and legislation. Less often, we see the names Ford, Lilly, and Kellogg—foundations which have granted money to support library programs of one sort or another.

How can you target grant-making agencies which have supported library programs in the past? How can you be sure these sources are interested in funding your program? This is where the curiosity and tenacity of a dedicated librarian come into play. How better to use your skills than to help yourself and your library program?

GENERAL SOURCES

The *Bowker Annual of Library and Book Trade Information* is the obvious source of information about funding which is directly applicable to libraries. Each year there is a summary of the current status of funding through such programs as the Library Services Construction Act (LSCA), Title I, Title II, and Title III; the Education Consolidation and Improvement Act of 1981 (ECIA), chapter 2; the Higher Education Act (HEA), Title IIA, Title IIB and IIC; the National Endowment for the Humanities (NEH), and the National Historical Publications and Records Commission.

Do not stop with the *Bowker Annual*. It describes only legislation and federal programs which have historically supported libraries. If you are in a vocational/technical school, you should look for sources that provide money for that specialty, such as Fund for the Improvement of Post-Secondary Education or the Vocational Education Act. Your library may have a special collection which you wish to catalog and publicize, or you may want to participate in a job exchange. Granting agencies, other than those summarized by *Bowker*, meet a wide variety of needs.

The *Annual Register of Grant Support* (published by Marquis) is a standard reference work on nonrepayable financial support: grant programs of government agencies, public and private foundations, corporations, community trusts, unions, educational and professional associations, and special-interest organizations. The *Register*'s four indexes provide access by subject, organization and program, geographical location, and personnel.

FEDERAL GOVERNMENT

Published annually by the Office of Management and Budget (OMB), the *Catalog of Federal Domestic Assistance* is a government-wide compendium of federal programs and activities that give both financial and nonfinancial assistance. It identifies types of assistance, eligibility requirements, program uses and restrictions, agency procedures, and guidelines for the application and award process, along with federal program policies and regulations. Information about the support programs is cross-referenced by functional classification, subject, applicants, deadlines for applications, popular names, authorizing legislation, and federal circular requirements.

Two daily federal publications (to which the *Catalog* refers its readers) are the *Commerce Business Daily* and the *Federal Register.* The *CBD* lists U.S. government procurement invitations, research and development requests, and contract awards. The *Federal Register* provides rules, regulations, and legal notices issued by federal agencies (as well as proposed rules) and notices of meetings and hearings. The *Catalog* will refer you to one of these daily publications for deadline dates, amendments to funding programs, notices of awards, and other current information. For example, although final regulations for the ECIA-2 programs were published in the July 29, 1982 *Federal Register,* the regulations were disapproved by Congress, and revised final regulations were published in the November 19, 1982 *Federal Register.*

FOUNDATIONS

Now we turn to foundations. The *Foundation Grants Index,* published by the Foundation Center, indicates the kinds of grants foundations have supported in the past. This reference book will tell you who might be receptive to your idea. It is a detailed summary of grants given by large private or community foundations. The 1983 *Index* summarizes 27,121 grant records, totaling over $1.49 billion, given by 444 large foundations. The grants (at least $5,000) were given to organizations, rather than individuals. Each foundation is listed alphabetically by state and records of the foundations' grants of $5,000 or more are arranged alphabetically by recipient. Five indexes are available: an alphabetical index of names of recipients, an alphabetical index of key words and phrases (referring to the grant description or type of recipient organization), subject categories (subdivided by recipient location), a recipient category index, and an alphabetical index of the foundations and their addresses.

The *Foundations Directory,* also published by the Foundation Center, is the standard reference work for information about nongovernmental foundations in the United States. The ninth edition (published in 1983) includes 4,063 foundations, with assets of $47.5 billion. The large foundations in the *Foundation Grants Index* are included in this reference book, along with many smaller granting sources.

Arranged alphabetically by state, the entries provide the foundations' name, address, and telephone number; names of donors; a brief statement of purpose (including special limitations); financial data such as assets, gifts received, expenditures, total grants, number of grants paid, and highest and lowest grants; names of officers and trustees; and grant-application information.

The four indexes to the *Directory* provide access by state and city, foundation names, personnel, and fields of interest. Foundations listed in boldface type under a field of interest make grants on a national or regional basis, while the others generally limit their giving to the city or state in which they are located. Looking under "libraries" in the fields-of-interest index, you will find only fourteen foundations in boldface type; under "vocational education" there are seven; under "secondary education" there are 157. Under "adult education" there are only three.

Foundation Center Source Book Profiles, also published by the Foundation Center, provides detailed information on the large grant-making foundations in the United States which operate on a regional or national basis. Information includes basic descriptive and fiscal information on the foundation; a statement on the policies, programs, and application procedures; and full listing of recent grants that are illustrative of current programs. It is indexed by foundation name, subject, location, and type of support.

The seventh edition of the *National Data Book* (also published by the Foundation Center) gives brief financial profiles of nearly 22,000 active foundations in the United States, many of which are not listed in the *Foundations Directory.* This information is arranged alphabetically by state. For further information about a foundation listed in this resource, you may write to the foundation directly or consult the Internal Revenue Service information returns which are filed annually by all private foundations. The IRS information returns give full listings of grants made by the foundations in the year of record. The index is arranged alphabetically by the name of the foundations.

In addition to the abovementioned volumes, separate directories are published about the foundations in a particular state or region. A bibliography of these resources is in the *National Data Book*.

The Foundation Center offers still more help to the money hunter. COMSEARCH Printouts are computer-prepared guides to foundation giving. In addition, a list of nationwide foundation reference collections (for free public use) is available in each publication issued by the Foundation Center. Also, the Center operates libraries in New York City and Washington, D.C., which contain all public records and printed publications relating to private foundations. Field offices, with extensive collections, are in Cleveland and San Francisco. Seventy-eight cooperating collections are available in all fifty states, Mexico, Puerto Rico, and the Virgin Islands.

CORPORATIONS

Corporations may be approached to fund ideas that will give them good publicity and may be viewed as beneficial to their employees. Few corporations make grant guidelines available, nor do they publicize philanthropic objectives or procedures for grant applicants to follow. In 1982, corporate contributions were only 1.77 percent of their pretax net income; however, "corporations have donated the largest percentage of their grants to education in the last four years."[2]

While money may be obtained from corporations, the probability of "gifts" to the local or university library, such as books, technical materials, or equipment, should not be overlooked. This is especially true if the local corporate managers work closely with a college or department of a local university. These managers often have an opportunity to determine such gifts.

As a librarian, you should be aware of special alignments between departments or colleges and local business and industry. This may give you an opportunity to discuss special needs with professors and deans, which can be presented to local businesses and industries.

INDIVIDUALS

A nonprofit organization, such as Friends of the Library and individual citizens, should not be overlooked as other sources of revenue.

---

2. Robert Lefferts, *Getting a Grant in the Nineteen Eighties: How to Write Successful Grant Proposals,* 2nd ed. (Englewood Cliffs, N.J.: Prentice-Hall, 1982).

Most public and school libraries cannot sell their inventory for profit, but they can donate such things as duplicate and out-of-date titles to nonprofit organizations. Friends of the Library, in turn, can hold a book sale and return their profits to the library.

If Friends of the Library assures you of a certain level of funding for the year, this should be put into the regular budget as a "source of income." However (as is often the case), you cannot honestly project this amount. Therefore it can (and should) be planned and handled as if it were an exceptional source of funds.

Contributions from individuals can also be solicited. It is helpful to have an established program by which a person who has died can be remembered by friends through book purchases. Bookplates can be prepared in his or her name.

Strategy

Now that you know the available resources, what strategy should you use? In general, the government funds what has been done before, is likely to continue funding an ongoing and successful program, and is likely to give funding extensions. It is also likely to give "seed grants" for various ideas. Foundations, on the other hand, like to fund new and innovative ideas and like to know that programs, once begun, will need no more support.

When you look for federal assistance, be sure you know who administers the funds. For instance, you will save yourself time by noting that LSCA funds are administered by state and territorial library administrative agencies. By talking directly with a consultant at your state library, you can get all program and funding information from someone close to home.

In no case should you hesitate to telephone a grant-making source for information, instructions, feedback, suggestions, and evaluation of your program idea.

Recognizing that corporations respond to local needs, you may want to become aware of the interests of their presidents or chief executive officers. An officer who enjoys hunting is more likely to support a collection of books on guns than a collection on antique cars.

After you have discovered the personal interests of the CEO or the chairman of the board (and prepared a grant proposal), you should approach the corporation at its highest level. All philanthropic decisions are made at the top. All the rules about grant-proposal writing pertain, but it is especially important to define how the corporation will create a good public image as a result of its contribution. For this reason, it is often better to ask a corporation to provide money for equipment than for a program. It is also important to emphasize benefits which might accrue to employees (even retired employees) of the business.

It is with local contributions in mind that all Foundation Center publications are arranged by state. People who live in New York, Washington, D.C., or Illinois have many granting sources available to them. Those who live in New Mexico, Arkansas, or Mississippi might better turn to the *Source Book,* which lists the large foundations that operate on a regional or national basis; the *National Data Book,* which lists the small foundations; or the *Annual Register of Grant Support,* which lists a variety of granting agencies.[3]

PRACTICE EXPERIENCES

1. Identify a source of funding and request that it send you its agency's proposal requirements.

2. List the major sources of federal money for public libraries and the agencies through which you might gain access to such funds.

3. Using the three major reference resources mentioned in the text, identify possible funding sources for construction purposes, for acquisition, for staff training.

4. List the major sources of federal money for school libraries and the agencies through which you might gain access to them.

5. Enumerate other reference resources that list funding agencies.

SELECTED READINGS

Annual Register of Grant Support: 1983–84. 17th ed. Chicago: Marquis, 1983.
Commerce Business Daily. U.S. Department of Commerce.
Federal Register. Washington, D.C., National Archives and Records Service.
Foundation Directory. 9th ed. New York: The Foundation Center, 1983.
Foundation Grants Index. 12th ed. New York: The Foundation Center, 1983.

3. *Annual Register of Grant Support: 1983–84,* 17th ed. (Chicago: Marquis, 1983), p.xii.

Gaby, Patricia V., and Daniel M. Gaby. *Nonprofit Organizational Handbook: A Guide to Fundraising, Grants, Lobbying, Membership Building, Publicity and Public Relations.* Englewood Cliffs, N.J.: Prentice-Hall, 1979.

Goldstein, Sherry E., ed. *Foundation Center Source Book Profiles, Series 4.* New York: The Foundation Center, 1980.

Proposal Writers' Swipe File III: 15 Professionally Written Grant Proposals in Prototypes of Approaches, Styles, and Structures. Washington, D.C.: Taft Corp., 1981.

7
Writing the Budget Presentation

Why Is Writing So Critical?

You must take responsibility for your message being received and understood by the funding board or agency. Presenting program ideas and their costs, while leaving it up to your reader to draw conclusions, is irresponsible, and may be ineffective. You must know why your programs exist, how they are important to the community, and how many people they affect *before* you face your board of trustees and funding agency.

This chapter will present:

Sample budget presentations for line-item and program budgets

Strategies for consideration when you write budget presentations.

Also, you will be asked to:

Question the intentions of sample presentations
Write your explanations of budgeted items

You must know who is going to read your budget presentation and what they are looking for. Funding boards or agencies always have less money to distribute than is requested by the agencies they fund. Therefore, they look at both the budgetary proposals and the benefits provided the clientele. They weigh the importance to the community of updating fire-fighting equipment versus a new book-mobile, of increasing the police force or adding a children's librarian,

89

of meeting the utility costs of the city's schools and your request for five study carrels and four slide carousels.

Each funding board or agency has an informal, unstated idea of giving each requesting institution its "fair share," but the need for physical safety and comfort always prevails. Only after the basic physical needs are met can funding agencies begin to consider programs designed to foster self-actualization of the people. As frustrating as this is to a library director, it is better to recognize that life-supporting agencies will always get a larger share of the pie than the library.

But there are things you can do to make your share as large as it can be. As library director, you are responsible for the adequate funding of your program. You must be sure that your program is meeting real needs of a large part of your community and that you can demonstrate this to others through facts, figures, and persuasion.

Your community profile, library statistics, and library performance measures should prepare you with facts and your budget will prepare you with figures. Now you need to write a persuasive presentation.

Strategy

You cannot consistently ask for more than you can get. If you do, you'll lose credibility with the funding agency. You must "read the signs" of political realities. Often, a city or school administration will request that the budget reflect no more than a 2 or 10 percent increase. Today, more likely, the trend is to *reduce* the budget by 2 or 10 percent.

On the other hand, don't shortchange your budget. Realize that there are definite roles that people in the funding process are expected to play. When someone steps outside his or her role, the whole process is jeopardized. There are boards of trustees that, instead of advocating a library's budget, cut it. Then the budget, already trimmed of all fat, is presented to the funding agency, which, as a matter of course, cuts it again.

It is easier for a board or funding agency to cut items which are listed separately. For example, if you lump all library supplies together with the book budget in a Materials and Supplies line item, you will be less likely to run out of money to buy charge cards and overdue notices. If you itemize supplies, the funding agency may be tempted to take issue with some of your specific needs.

If you know the budget will be cut, it may be better to lump items together so that the cut will be across the board and decisions about how to spend the remaining money are yours. Once the funding agency tells you to cut the money in your Equipment line, which would have been spent on a new microfilm cabinet, but leaves you the money to buy a microfilm reader, you cannot buy the cabinet instead, because the reader is of no use to you without storage for the film. It is wise to establish priorities on the equipment you need. If you share that information with the funding agency, it is more likely to cut items you feel are less vital, instead of using its amateur judgment. Remember:

> You can have two or three items which are priority 1.
> You have to justify the need for all new equipment.

Don't assume that, because you have set priorities on equipment items, the board will agree with you.

Identify the administrators who seem to be most successful in getting their budgets passed as requested—the administrators and programs which seem to have the confidence of the funding agency. Study them and their budget presentations and learn what you can from them. You may find that one has a politically astute clientele, and that another's clientele makes up the majority of the community. On the other hand, a third administrator's success may result from something as simple as having accurately guessed what he or she was likely to get and having asked for only slightly more. In this case, the ratio of request to appropriation is high.

Be aware of the difficulty which may arise if you want to eliminate a program in order to decrease your budget. Branch libraries occasionally are not cost effective, but political realities may be such that stopping their services would anger enough citizens to influence next year's appropriation negatively. There may be programs you have to maintain, against your better judgment, because your clientele (or a member of your funding agency) wants them.

Be aware, also, of what program(s) your community supports. The school board in an Eastern town cut a teacher's position to meet the budgetary constraints required by the town's finance committee. During a town meeting, the residents voted to reinstate that money in the budget. Thus a shrewd administrator can use community support to get full funding, even while he or she plays the game required by the officials.

Basics of the Written Budget Presentation

LINE-ITEM BUDGET
The line-item format is often such that a three-year history is made available to the funding agency, citing the

Amount appropriated and spent the previous year
Amount requested, appropriated, and spent during the current year
Amount requested for the next year

Line-item budgets are expected to be incremental—to increase a bit each year to reflect rising costs. Since the items on each line of the budget are not tied in to any programs or services, neither their rationale nor their effectiveness is questioned.

The budget presentation need explain only the percentage increase of each item, and special attention need be paid only to items which increase more than the expected percent. Special attention should also be given to explaining any decrease in an item. You don't have to treat increases or decreases equally. Focus on the issues that are politically salable.

LINE-ITEM PRESENTATION
Using the line-item budget sheets in figure 22, we'll hypothesize the fiscal year 1983 request. The guidelines allow for a 5 percent across-the-board salary increase, a 5 percent increase in supplies, and a 25 percent increase in light and heat. The budget is not to exceed a 7 percent increase.

Noticeable changes in the line items result from the proposed purchase of an IBM personal computer for the use of patrons. As a result of this one-time capital outlay, you plan to maintain the acquisition budget as is, although $2,500 will be shifted from print to nonprint to allow you to purchase at least five software packages. The training budget increases 43 percent to bring the staff up to date. All other increases conform with the guidelines; so your presentation might look like this:

I. With a 7 percent increase, the library will
    A. Provide a 5 percent across-the-board increase to staff
    B. Purchase a computer for use by patrons
    C. Purchase a minimum of 5 software programs for use by patrons
    D. Train the library staff to use and teach the use of the computer
    E. Maintain the acquisition budget at its present level
II. Access to a computer will
    A. Answer the requests we received from 70 percent of our adult patrons through a survey conducted in January

   B. Reinforce its everyday usefulness to the parents of
      students who are learning to use computers in school
   C. Allow students who do not have home computers
      to do their homework
   D. Become a training ground for adults who wish to
      become computer literate
III. The provided software programs will
   A. Offer the services requested by adults who an-
      swered the survey: word processing, language
      learning, and budgeting
IV. Training the library staff will
   A. Prepare them for the new technology
   B. Allow staff to teach prospective users to use the
      computer
   C. Assure that a trained person is available at all times
V. Maintaining the acquisition budget at its current level
   will
   A. Decrease the number of titles purchased and pro-
      cessed by 15%
   B. Increase the time technical services staff can spend
      learning and training patrons to use the computer
   C. Be consistent with the library's statistics, which show
      a decline in circulation of print materials

PROGRAM BUDGET

The program budget format provides the opportunity for you to
describe the various programs, with their key goals and objectives.
Typically, you can present the most cost effective/efficient strategies
for achieving those outcomes and build a powerful case for accept-
ance of your requests. Alternatives for fulfilling the goals and objectives do not need to be exhaustive, and a shrewd presenter would
use them only to contrast the more positive results to be obtained
by the recommended strategies and requested funding levels.

One of the most effective methods is to highlight changes in existing and new programs in the main text. Established programs which
are not changing (except through approved incremental increases)
can be assumed to be approved and therefore noncontroversial.

Presenting program priorities and the funds needed to support
each is a final step in preparing the written presentation for program
budgeting. This can be a tabular chart, which can easily be scanned
by the reader, but it must accurately summarize the recommended
programs and levels of funding for each (see figure 23).

Account Number	Account Title	Actual Expenditures, FY '80	Actual Expenditures, FY '81	Appropriation, FY '82	Actual Expenditures through Dec. '82	Estimated Expenditures, FY '82	Requested for FY '83
100	Personal services	259,447	267,231	280,592	140,296	280,592	294,622
300	Materials & supplies	70,611	72,729	76,366	38,396	74,324	76,795
400	Contractual services	45,669	47,034	49,386	25,511	49,386	59,554
500	Lease/purchase	2,000	2,060	2,075	1,038	2,075	2,137
600	Capital outlay	1,826	1,882	2,063	—	0	6,294
Total		379,553	390,936	410,482	205,241	406,377	439,402
100	Personal services	259,447	267,231	280,592	140,296	280,592	294,622
310	Print materials	60,908	62,736	65,875	31,046	63,883	63,375
320	Nonprint	1,770	1,870	1,914	1,800	1,914	4,414
330	Office	3,272	3,375	3,538	1,500	3,488	3,715
335	Custodial	1,947	2,000	2,160	2,000	2,160	2,268
340	Electrical	1,770	1,775	1,914	1,200	1,914	2,010
345	Plumbing	708	730	765	650	765	803
350	Safety	236	243	200	200	200	210
Total		70,611	72,729	76,366	38,396	74,324	76,795

405	Postage	1,104	1,137	1,472	1,472	1,472	1,693
410	Telephone	1,922	1,998	2,078	1,039	2,078	2,390
415	Light & heat	25,464	26,209	28,239	14,120	28,239	35,299
420	Water	295	303	319	160	319	351
430	Printing	1,123	1,100	1,012	400	1,012	1,063
435	Microfilm	1,121	1,208	1,212	1,000	1,212	1,273
440	Binding	826	853	891	290	891	936
445	Auto. maint.	110	110	120	60	120	132
450	Leased equip.	564	588	612	306	612	673
455	Bldg. maint.	12,685	13,060	13,018	6,509	13,018	14,320
460	Training	354	364	304	100	304	1,304
470	Service contracts	101	104	109	55	109	120
	Total	45,669	47,034	49,386	25,511	49,386	59,554
510	Computer	—	—	—	—	—	—
520	Copy machine	1,200	1,236	1,296	648	1,296	1,335
530	Stationwagon	800	824	779	390	779	802
	Total	2,000	2,060	2,075	1,038	2,075	2,137
610	Furniture	—	800	114	0	0	0
615	Equipment	1,249	441	1,294	0	0	6,294
620	AV Equip.	577	641	655	0	0	0
	Total	1,826	1,882	2,063	0	0	6,294

Figure 22. Line-Item Budget for Submission (Dollars)

	Computer Literacy	Acquisitions	Total
Personal services	$36,816	$29,453	$ 66,269
Materials & supplies	2,500	65,289	67,789
Contractual services	1,500	--	1,500
Capital outlay	5,000	--	5,000
Total	$45,816	$94,742	$140,558

Figure 23. Program Budget for Submission

PROGRAM PRESENTATION

If we use the same data in the line-item budget, the computer literacy and acquisitions programs could be presented as follows:

Computer literacy has become as important as learning to read. The need has been identified through a survey distributed to adult library users in January. To meet this need, the library will

1. Purchase a personal computer for patrons to use in the library by September 1983
2. Purchase software packages requested by adults who answered a survey: word processing, spread sheet, and language training by September 1983
3. Train all 30 library staff members to use the computer by October 1983
4. Schedule biweekly use classes for groups of no more than 6 adults no later than November 1983, to be taught by reference and technical service librarians
5. Schedule 4 hours every afternoon for students, no later than October 1983

By maintaining the acquisition budget at the same level, we will

1. Purchase 15 percent fewer print titles during fiscal year 1983
2. Purchase software packages by September 1983
3. Decrease staff needed to process print titles by 12.5 FTE
4. Free 12.5 FTE staff to train themselves and others to use the computer by October 1983

General Goals

You must write a brief, concise, and interesting account of the library's budgetary needs. To meet these criteria, the presentation should be

> Well organized
> In outline format
> Visually pleasing.

Staff Input

Once the presentation is written, share it with members of your staff. Since they probably know more about the library than members of the funding agency, and are "tuned into" some of the misconceptions held by the public, they can critique your presentation in a helpful way.

Ask your staff to identify words which are used by librarians but often are meaningless to the public. You may be too close to library jargon to recognize them. Examples are:

jobber	machine-readable data	serials
periodicals	YA programming	OCLC
cataloging	com catalog	retrospective conversion
classification	shelflist	reconciliation of serials holdings
serials checklist	bibliographic tools	searching

By opening yourself to the questions of your staff, you will be able to plug holes and delete and add information which will make your presentation persuasive.

Both the accomplishments and limitations of the library's programs should be addressed in the written proposal. This may be the only time of the year that the funding agency (as well as your staff) recognizes the strides made by the organization and the part they play. A morale builder for your staff, the presentation may solicit ongoing interest from members of the funding board or agency.

Since you will have the opportunity to supplement your written presentation with a verbal one, write briefly and clearly. You will be able to expand on the documentation during your in-person presentation.

PRACTICE EXPERIENCES

1. Using your library's budget format, write a presentation for two line items or two programs.

2. Pretend you are a member of the funding board, and attack the two budget presentations in this chapter. What questions will you ask the library director during his or her verbal presentation?

3. Rewrite the budget presentations to address your critics. Consider future costs and plans, if you feel that would be appropriate.

4. Maintaining the acquisitions budget at its present level is fairly unusual. What risks might this approach run? What benefit might accrue?

SELECTED READINGS

Burkhead, Jesse, and Paul Bringewatt. *Municipal Budgetline: A Primer for Elected Officials*. Washington, D.C.: Joint Center for Political Studies, 1974.

Lefferts, Robert. *How to Prepare Charts and Graphs for Effective Reports*. New York: Harper, 1982.

8
In-Person Presentations

In-person presentations by organizational subunits are often required to provide the formal decision makers with face-to-face information about budget proposals. These presentations are often called "budget hearings" or "budget reviews." Usually, you might expect to have two levels of such hearings: one with your own board and one with the review unit of your parent organization. Such encounters provide an excellent opportunity for you to make a good case for your library budget. There are many fears and frustrations for all managers as a result of these reviews, but there are methods which can not only reduce the fear and frustration but help you be an effective spokesperson for the library and its functions in the organization.

This chapter will suggest ideas and approaches you might take to gain approval of the library budget.

Presenting your budget proposal to a decision-making board allows you to benefit from personal contact and two-way communication. This is your opportunity to

> Ensure that the board understands your program and your funding needs
> Provide details and address the doubts of board members
> Influence the decision makers.

Anticipating the In-Person Oral Presentation

You need to gather important background information before your presentation:

When will you be heard?
Where will you be heard?
What will your time constraints be?
Who is your audience?
What are the board's expectations regarding the presentation?
Are there rules or traditions you should know about?
What will happen before and after your presentation?

Most of the time, answers to these questions are not volunteered by those who arrange the meetings. You may want to attend presentations made by other department heads or you may rely on your contacts to give you the "inside information" you need.

Timing Is Everything

You may not be given a choice of hearing time or place, but it won't hurt to request what is best for you. If there is a comfortable meeting room in the library, invite the board to your territory. In this way you gain control of the timing and the comfort of your audience.

By bringing the board to the library, you can give the members a tour of the facilities, thereby bringing your programs and needs to light in a special way. In addition, you can arrange the meeting room to your liking, eliminating intimidating aspects, and you can ensure everyone's comfort.

Advertising executives, trying to sell their campaigns to prospective clients, try to make their presentation either first or last—either of which ensures a memorable presentation. Of course, if you are not well prepared, you *won't want* to be remembered.

If you are allotted 9:45 to 10:00 p.m. on a week night, you would prepare a different presentation than if you were given a 9:45 to 10:00 a.m. hearing. The hearings may begin at 7 p.m., and as the evening wears on and the preceding hearings exceed their scheduled time slots, *your* hearing may be delayed until close to midnight. By that time, of course, you will confront a tired and irritated audience. Thus a concise, interesting, and entertaining presentation will be a necessity.

Since this is your chance to explain and persuade, you must assess your audience. Find out who they are.

Are they or their families library users?
Do they have children in school, or in the pre-school story hour?

What areas of town do they live in?
Which school or branch library will they have a personal interest in?
To which interests of theirs can you appeal?

Also, assess how much they know about the library, their beliefs and values, their attitudes toward you and the library program.

During your presentation you will appeal to both the intellect and the emotions of the funding board. Try to persuade them of your need by appealing to their logic, but appeal also to their

> Pride ("If we launch this program, we will be one of twenty libraries in the forefront of a trend that will sweep the nation.")
>
> Competitiveness ("You'll be shocked to learn that ours is the only library in the state without a telephone.")
>
> Indignation ("Are we going to sit here and do nothing while our competitor lures our patrons away?")

These examples further emphasize the need to know the value and belief systems of your audience.

If you are addressing a group of nonreaders, who see budgets as no more than ploys to take money from their pockets, you should have a more formal and persuasive presentation than if the group values education and sees budgeting as a tool for better management of a motherhood–and–apple-pie institution. Obviously, these are two extremes—but probably both extremes will be *represented* on your decision-making board or in your parent organization.

You need to determine, both formally and informally, what rules and traditions have been observed within the organization during presentations. Usually you can find out about formal rules by asking your immediate superior. However, it is well to remember that, in addition to formal rules, traditions or customs have often developed within the organization as a part of these public processes. Some of them relate to how to address various persons, where to sit or stand, or if it's okay to have staff members present to help answer questions.

There are two ways to obtain such information, both of which should be used. Inquire of one of your inside, informal sources and attend presentations by other units of the parent organization. Use the information and observations to help you with *your* presentation plans.

It is also helpful to know what usually happens before and after your presentation. How much material do you need to provide the hearing group in advance? Are there informal discussions which should or must be carried out? With whom and when? Are you expected to initiate follow-up discussions and provide additional information? The people to answer such questions are the same as those cited above: your immediate superior and your informal contacts.

Organizing Your Presentation

Since your purpose is to inform and persuade, you need to master the deductive, inductive, and eliminative methods of organizing your presentation.

Deductive reasoning moves forward from a statement or premise which must be accepted as true by everyone you are talking with. This premise is used together with facts or other premises to develop particular arguments or plans of action.

Be careful in choosing a premise on which to base your presentation. Librarians often feel that the importance of education, reading, and libraries is self-evident. They may begin budget presentations by stating that "libraries are basic to one's happiness." Unfortunately, this premise does not have unanimous support. Indeed, its support may be in inverse relation to budgetary demands of life-sustaining institutions (i.e., police and fire departments).

Since deductive reasoning moves from generalization to specifics, the line-item, incremental budget is a good candidate for deductive presentation. Whether the budgetary guidelines limit you to a 10 percent increase or require a 3 percent decrease is a premise on which you should build your presentation. If you act on this premise, your argument will be persuasive. The line-item budget is easy to defend, as long as you stay within the guidelines, because tradition expects increments.

As a school librarian, you might begin your deductive reasoning by stating: "The school library exists to support and supplement the school curriculum." It is hard to believe that anyone would disagree with that statement, but you may have to prove it before you gain consensus and can continue with your presentation. Once you are convinced that everyone agrees with that premise, you might explain that the curriculum expanded during the year to include creative writing, two foreign languages, and office management. "Therefore, we need $4,000 to buy materials to support these new curricula."

Inductive reasoning moves from specifics to create a generalization. Usually, this means building on a series of facts that result in a conclusion. Fact: "Circulation has increased 100 percent during this fiscal or school year." Fact: "Staff has decreased by 0.5 FTE during this fiscal or school year." Fact: "There is a two-week lag between the return of books to the library and their return to the shelves." Fact: "Accessibility of materials to users has decreased proportionately." Conclusion: "Pages must be hired to reshelve materials. This is the reason for a $700 increase in the circulation program."

Program budget formats are well suited to inductive presentations. By using program budgeting, you begin with a number of programs which create the entirety of the services offered by the library. By gaining support for each component, you establish that these programs are worth supporting. From those specifics, you can accumulate support for the whole.

You can picture the shape of this argument as a pyramid: you make a series of statements which, together, provide the base for the apex or conclusion.

Eliminative reasoning allows you to identify a problem, then address the alternative solutions, eliminating each until only one remains. You can fall into traps with this method if you have not considered *all* the alternatives and if their rejection is not clearly conceived. Alternative solutions usually have advantages *and* disadvantages. Sometimes one clearly outweighs the other, but all too often they depend on opinion, and the opinions of board members may differ from yours.

Visual Presentation

The most common presentation is a lecture. But because audiences retain only about 20 percent of what they hear, and 50 percent of what they see and hear, you will want to prepare visual aids: slides or a slide/tape presentation, charts and graphs on a chalkboard or flip chart, overhead transparencies, or a videotape. The room arrangement, equipment availability, and preparation time will determine which method(s) you use.

A slide/tape presentation requires the ability to darken and arrange the room for ease of viewing, requires equipment, and is time consuming in preparation. It is, on the other hand, an effective way of bringing library programs to life.

Charts and graphs require a wall or easel, and require little time to prepare. Moreover, you can focus your audience on the specifics you wish to highlight. If you use charts or graphs, be sure there is plenty of "white space." If you present a table, present no more than three or four columns per visual, and do not talk more than one minute with any one visual.

Overhead transparencies require an overhead projector and screen, and no more time to prepare than charts and graphs. Your presentation can be drawn, printed, or typed onto a piece of paper which can be made into a transparency by a photocopier. When you present word visuals, highlight what you say by using key words. Never use complete sentences. Use no more than seven words per line and limit the visual to eight lines. By following these rules of thumb you will ensure the necessary "white space."

As videotapes become common, they will be used more and more often during budget presentations. They require a darkened room, a particular seating arrangement, and special equipment, and can be time consuming to prepare. But this medium brings the life of the library to light by providing action.

Are There Any Questions?

You needn't flinch when you hear the moderator of the hearing board ask for questions. It's an opportunity, if you have done your homework.

"Yes, I have a question," says Mr. Brown. "I still don't see what will be gained from a deposit library at the rest home in the Heights."

Having done your homework, you know that Mr. Brown's mother-in-law lives in a different rest home, and you might respond this way: "Our survey of library users showed a lower representation from that home than others. We plan to pilot a deposit library in that home. If it's successful, we may be able to accommodate other homes in town."

"How many of your program participants are residents of this city?" asks Mr. Smith.

"I'm happy to report that the proportion of residents to out-of-towners has doubled since last year, Mr. Smith." Knowing that Mr. Smith does not want to support anyone outside his tax base, you have prepared for this question. (Be sure not to say *too* much.)

"What I want clarified," insists Mr. Jones, "is the meaning behind that flap I read about last month."

Don't assume you know what "that flap" refers to. Don't answer too quickly. "What flap, Mr. Jones? Was it something you read in a magazine?"

"No, no, no. I saw something about a library conference in the newspaper. It was held in Chicago. Why weren't you there?"

What started as a challenge can suddenly be turned to your advantage. "Yes, that *was* an excellent opportunity. I didn't attend because we had no travel funds. I've recommended a travel budget this year of $600. Luckily, the conference will be nearer home and I'll be able to attend and report back to you." By restating the question and having it clarified, you gain better understanding of the motive behind the question, as well as time to formulate a response.

"How exactly do the circulation figures compare between the high school and the junior high school?" demands Ms. Gray, the newest member of the funding board—a question you hadn't anticipated. Moreover, the statistics are not readily available. What do you say?

"I don't have those statistics handy, Ms. Gray. I'll pull them together and get them to you tomorrow." It is better to be straightforward (no apologies are necessary) than to respond uncertainly. A guess may mar credibility or raise more questions.

Why is Ms. Gray interested in those statistics? You might probe by asking: "Are you interested in any other data?" "No. I'm thinking that one way to cut our costs would be to shorten the hours of whichever library is used less."

This gives you information. Now you know her motive, and you can give her information regarding the in-library use of materials, the use of facilities, and the use of the reference staff, as well as the circulation figures. Your new board member needs to be oriented and educated about library uses and needs.

Besides identifying board members who need education, the question-and-answer period offers you a chance to witness an exchange of views among board members. You can learn a great deal about the individuals' values and assumptions through their group interaction. Every detail will make next year's presentation easier.

PRACTICE EXPERIENCES

1. Identify at least five important background-information items you should identify before you plan your in-person presentation.

2. Explain briefly why these are important for the presenter to understand.

3. Discuss the significance of formal and informal rules to the presenter.

4. Differentiate between inductive and deductive reasoning and explain how each might be used in a presentation.

5. Choose a visual presentation and, using that method, develop a portion of a presentation.

6. Discuss the in-person practices currently in use with your contact person in your parent organization. If you are a student, discuss this subject with a working librarian.

7. Without referring to the text, define deductive logic, inductive logic, and eliminative logic.

8. Summarize the budgetary formats that pertain to each of these three logical approaches.

9. Summarize the questions that must be answered while one prepares a budget presentation.

10. Summarize uses to which you can put a question-and-answer period.

SELECTED READINGS

Boettinger, Henry M. *Moving Mountains: Or the Art and Craft of Letting Others See Things Your Way*. New York: Macmillan, 1975.

Gronbeck, Bruce E. *The Articulate Person*. 2nd ed. Glenview, Ill.: Scott, Foresman, 1983.

Guth, Chester K., and Stanley S. Shaw. *How to Put on Dynamic Meetings: Teaming the Oral with the Visual*. Reston, Va.: Reston, 1980.

9
The Budget Cycle

It is July 1 and you are sitting in your office with a few free moments, away from all your duties as a library manager. This day marks the beginning of your new fiscal year: the implementation point for your newly approved budget and all the activities you have planned as part of that implementation. You have worked toward this fiscal year throughout most of last year, thinking, planning, evaluating, discussing issues and ideas, setting priorities for the library's program, and replanning what should and could be in your budget. Some of your most exciting dreams are dead, victims of budgetary limitations. You adjusted your expectations and goals many times, as you discovered the limitations of your parent organization to provide for them. However, a number of other significant goals and their supporting activities are firmly in place, having been hammered out and established through the budgeting process. You have the funds for them and reasonable expectations that they can be carried out.

You feel you have done a good job in preparation for this budget year. You also realize that, in the very near future, you will begin preparation for the budget to be implemented just a year from now. In your mind, you review the process by which budgets are established.

This scenario is representative of what all budget managers experience every year. The questions which rise out of such reflections go to the core of effective budgeting:

> Did I understand the budget cycle adequately?
> Did I work each portion sequentially to the best advantage?
> Did I use the previous years' experiences effectively?

Did I get the appropriate inputs from others at the right time?

Did I blend the exceptional sources of funding into the budget development effectively?

Did I develop and submit appropriate special-funding proposals?

Were my early projections of revenues supported by the final revenue allocations?

Do I understand better now, than I did a year ago, the politics of budgeting within my parent organization?

These and many other questions will occur to you as you ponder the information and budgeting skills you accumulate through study of this book. This chapter is a final overview of the budget cycle. Various steps of the process are covered extensively in other chapters, but here we bring all the issues together in a single overview/summary—a kind of map to follow in working through the budget cycle.

Figure 24 reviews the primary steps in budget development. This chapter deals with development of the budget, whereas the previous chapters focused on the planning processes necessary for that development. (The earlier chapters also dealt with the skills significant to these processes.) The budgeting process is interrelated with the planning process (as can be seen in Figure 24), and will be discussed in this chapter. (Figure 24 also identifies the chapters which deal with the steps of budget preparation.) Figure 25 identifies typical time lines associated with development of the budget as it relates to the fiscal year of an organization.

You have already learned a great deal about budget-planning processes. Now you will learn about the cycle of activities into which they fit.

The budgeting cycle is best looked at in reverse—that is, from the end result backward, to how that result was achieved. These final products and their specific dates in a calendar year "drive" all the other time lines of the cycle. Usually, the parent organization's final budget is approved within one month before the end of the current fiscal year; therefore, only eleven months are available beforehand for all of the budget cycle activities. Also, since the library is only one of a number of units in the parent organization's total budget, there must be time for *their* input before the organization itself seeks final budget approval. Therefore, approval of the library's budget, as a subunit of the parent organization, can reasonably be expected from one to four months before the approval of the parent organization's final budget. That interval gives the larger organization's planners time to compile all of the subunit budgets.

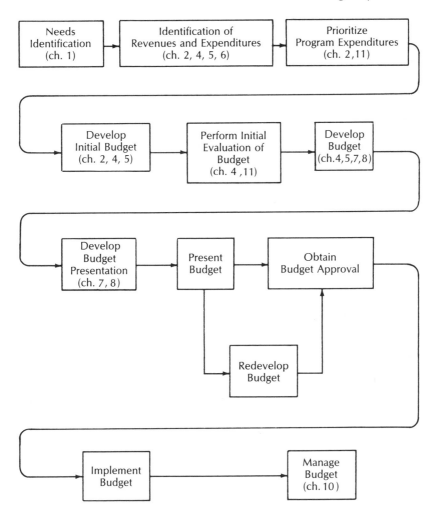

Figure 24. Budget Cycle Flow Chart

Figure 25 shows the steps—in reverse—of the critical elements of the process which leads to approval of the library budget.

Figure 26 places these elements in the order they are carried out during the year. Let's look briefly at the activities which form the budget cycle.

The needs assessment process (discussed in depth in chapter 1) is the core of your budget ideas, because it involves your study of the library as a set of systems and programs which interrelate and provide

Activity	Time
Budget implementation and management	1st day of new fiscal year
Parent organization's final budget approval	Last month of old fiscal year
Library budget approval	1 to 4 months before end of fiscal year
Library budget presentation	2 to 5 months before end of fiscal year
Budget redevelopment	Preceding 2 weeks
Budget presentation development	Preceding 4 weeks
Initial evaluation of budget	Preceding 2 weeks
Initial budget development	Preceding 4 weeks
Prioritizing of program expenditures	Preceding 4 weeks
Identification of revenues and expenditures	Preceding 4 weeks
Needs analysis	Preceding 8 weeks

Figure 25. Critical Steps in a Library Budget's Approval (in Reverse)

the foundation for rational analysis of your budget. It is during needs assessment that patrons and their needs are taken into account. Also during this time, employees and coworkers in the library have a chance to make initial formal inputs into the subsequent year's budget. You are challenged to look critically at the entire library function from the "needs" point of view so you will not (inadvertently) omit anything from your planning.

Needs, as a step in budget development, must be assessed very early in the budget year. As can be seen in the list of activities and dates in figure 25, the ideal is that this activity be carried out by the end of the second month of the fiscal year. In practice (depending on when the library budget is presented), the time frame might extend to the end of the third or the middle of the fourth month. It cannot be pushed much beyond, or the remainder of the system would be severely compressed. The more time taken by needs assessment (or any other activity), the less time will be available to perform the other activities—with the concomitant danger that inadequate time may result in inadequate planning.

As you may realize, needs assessment is not a solo activity on your part, but a highly interactive information-gathering and analysis activity over which you exert control and direction as the library manager. It is one step in the budget cycle where the experiences of the

Activity	Month of Fiscal Year											
	1	2	3	4	5	6	7	8	9	10	11	12
Needs ID	–	–	–									
Prioritizing			–	–								
R. & E. ID				–	–							
Develop initial budget					–	–						
Evaluate initial budget						–						
Develop budget		–	–	–	–	–	–					
Develop budget presentation							–	–				
Present budget								–				
Redevelop budget								–	–			
Obtain budget approval									–	–	–	–
Implement budget												–
Manage budget												–

Figure 26. Yearly Budget Activities Cycle

current year and the previous years are brought to bear on predicting and planning the future. Inadequacies in the system, imbalances in expenditure categories, inappropriate personnel deployment, and the need for changes are possible issues for inclusion in needs analysis.

Another important issue in needs assessment is that both formal and informal systems are at work. Input is obtained through formal systems designed to legitimize that input. Such systems include structured meetings, surveys, evaluations of activities, reports, and the like. But informal systems are at work as well, through informal discussions, chance remarks, political observations, and the like. Neither system can be considered completely structured or rational; therefore, there is a good deal of sifting to do when you receive input from either source.

Once you have clearly in mind what you believe your needs and priorities are, you are ready to test reality and see what you might expect in revenues to meet these needs. What might these needs cost and what funds might be available to meet them? As indicated in Figure 24, the chapters to review to understand this step and carry it out effectively are 2, 4, 5, and 6. (These chapters also explain the skills necessary to this second phase of the budget cycle.) It is during phase two that you bring together the pieces of information which define the scope of your potential budget. Obviously, if significant revenues are expected to come to the library through exceptional sources (as described in chapter 6), you will identify them at this time and include them as part of your budget development and presentation. (They usually result in reducing your requests for parent-organization budget funds.)

At this time, you want to develop your information as fully as possible, including the maximums in both revenues and potential expenditures. Now you are dreaming and scheming, and it is advisable not to be overly constrictive in your thinking. In a few months the limitations of reality will come upon you, but, just now, don't let that hamper your plans, since it is not unusual for creative and productive ideas to emerge from this stage of budget development.

Step 3 of figure 24 indicates that you now perform the first stage, prioritizing the potential programs. (The methods for doing this are covered in some detail in chapters 2 and 11.) Prioritizing is a method of analyzing the potential significance of the various activities you would like to see in the library operation, and your program budget has provided the categories for these activities. As you prioritize them, some questions must be answered:

> Without which programs would the library cease to function? These are your top priorities.
> Which other programs serve the greatest needs of the groups of library patrons. These are your next priorities.
> Which programs may be vital to significant political forces in the library service community? These must be considered high priorities.
> Which programs have great public visibility for library patrons? These also would be high priorities.

The real question is how to analyze the importance of the programs, but there is no easy answer for appropriate prioritization. Part of that answer lies in your ability to understand the fiscal/political realities of the parent organization and the community. There are various people from whom you can gain insight into these issues: long-term library employees, decision makers in the parent organization, community library committees, state library personnel. These people should be included in the process, as they can provide important information for you at this time.

However, when it comes to the final prioritization, you alone must make the decisions about the relative merits of the programs and their importance to the directions in which you believe the library should move. You are deciding about library functions that, you have concluded, are the most important in your community. You are thereby choosing directions for the library through these decisions. You are creating the kind of organization and services which have been conceived as most productive for the budget year, given all the influences (positive and negative) which you can identify at this time.

The Trial Budget

Now is the time to put the actual budget together in its first-draft form. (Chapters 2, 4, and 5 explain the skills for this task.) Additionally, it is at this time that a comparison should be made between the current-year budget and your actual expenditures. In this way you can begin to compensate, in the new budget, for shifts in your current operational year. Once the program priorities have been set and the resources and expenditures identified, producing the budget may be accomplished simply by using a sheet similar to figure 27. The programs are listed along one side of the chart and the line items along the other, and the blanks are completed by transferring the amounts from each program budget sheet, for each line item, to the appropriate box in the chart. After this the lines and columns

Programs	Line Items												Total Local Programs	Total Special Programs
Line-item totals														Grand Totals

Figure 27. Program Budget Recap Sheet

are totaled. By adding the totals, first down each line-item column and then across the program totals, you cross-check the totals. The horizontal total and the vertical total should match, if your sums have been accurate for both sets of figures. If they do not, cross-check all the figures against the postings from the program budget sheets. Correct and sum again until they are identical.

These totals should be a close approximation of the ones you produced in your expenditure planning (unless you made major changes in your priorities). The result is a "trial budget," which you will evaluate further, which your staff can critique, and which you can share with your informal contacts within the parent organization (as well as with your next line supervisor in the parent organization). Your discussion at this point indicates to these persons that this is your first-run, needs-based projection, not your final budget proposal. It is a discussion document, designed to provide a way of responding to identified needs. However, you need to make it clear that the discussions, which will take place throughout the final approval of the budget, are an expected and needed part of the budgeting process.

The trial budget should be completed not later than the middle of the budget year, to give ample time for evaluation by appropriate people (as well as yourself). When the budget has been totaled for the first time, it may become obvious that adjustments have to be made, upward or downward.

The necessity of matching the proposed budget amounts to the projected expenditures and the projected revenues is absolute. When each amount has been summed, you can go back to your revenue projections and make comparisons. The "cut line" established by your maximum revenue projections (in actual dollars) becomes the final cut line of your prioritized list of programs and program costs. (A "cut line" is the point at which all of your expected revenues have been used up. See figure 40 in chapter 11.) In making this comparison, you can establish a tentative cut line before you get into your final budget development.

Initial Evaluation

The next step in the budget cycle is initial evaluation, in two parts: internal and external. The internal phase involves input and evaluation from you and your staff. It can be a very helpful reevaluation, since you now know the bottom line of your needs budget and can begin a review of the realities as you perceive them. (This often leads to a closer analysis of your dreams.) Do dreams have higher priorities than some of the programs? Are there alternative sources of funding which should be pursued, thereby reducing the local funding total by increasing the total monies in special funding? The internal evaluation helps you deal with the many challenges which must change the needs budget into the budget you will propose.

The other informal evaluation of the budget which is undertaken at this time is with your contact(s) in the parent organization. This person or persons can impart additional realities—how various items and plans in your needs budget may be viewed by the parent organization in its formal review. This information and these observations are fed back into your internal evaluation and considered as you move toward production of your actual budget.

It is also during this stage that information from the budgets of previous years becomes highly significant. Later, most people who will review the budget will look critically at patterns of expenditures which appear to be greatly different from those of the past few budgets. The more divergent from those budgets your proposal seems to be, the more critical the reviewers will be. It is therefore very important to use this information as suggested in chapter 7.

For instance, if you show a 25 percent increase in contract services over last year, you must be prepared, at the presentation, to explain how and why this happened. Such drastic changes almost always meet with criticism from reviewers. If changes have made such an increase obviously necessary, you will be on relatively safe ground if you include them in your budget (you have a built-in explanation). Again, if you had a copy machine under lease (contract services) for several years, and now plan to buy one, your budget will probably be reduced in contract services and increased in equipment. This is easily explained in just that manner—as a shift from one line item to another in order to achieve greater long-run economies.

Every line item in the budget must be considered with the same care. Apply whatever limits you have informally identified through your sources in the parent organization and identify the trouble spots, then evaluate each of them. Are there alternatives? Are such levels legitimate for library effectiveness? What do your informal advisors say?

Usually by this time in the budget year, the patterns and expectations of the parent organization have been firmly established through the political processes in which its decision makers have been involved. Therefore, you can refine what you have been developing so that it looks reasonable to you and your staff. As you determine which line items must be reduced to conform to probable approvable percentage increases (or decreases), you are forced to go back into each program budget and reevaluate.

Are there less costly alternatives which were not in the program budget the first time, which you and your staff might now be willing to consider to reduce the cost of that line-item? Are there readjustments between line items which might result in an appropriate shift in the line-item totals, making them more satisfactory? Could combinations of program personnel and costs be achieved to reduce total costs?

This type of internal reevaluation is a necessary part of the budgeting cycle, in order to bring the optimal services into line with the realities of the actual budget.

Preparing the Final Budget

You are now ready for serious budgeting. It seems like a long process, but it's effective, for you know the elements of each program, you understand the issues involved in accomplishing your objectives, and you have the data necessary to build a final budget which is both realistic and salable. In this two-month period, you will sort out the most critically needed programs and the most efficient means of providing them. These will be the basis of your final budget, whose development is a result of all the discussions and analyses (and you know that even after the formal presentation there may be further changes).

For the moment, you assemble all the parts into a final whole. (Figure 27 can be used again, as you work from the program-budget figures like those in chapters 2 and 3 and place the line-item amounts in the required places.) At this stage, you again pay particular attention to the percent of increase for each line item. Those above the formally recommended percentages of your parent organization will need special consideration as you develop your budget presentation. Also, the totals (bottom lines) for the whole budget should be analyzed again. The percentage increase (or decrease) from each line item of the current year's budget should be computed. Are these percentages within the prescribed or expected limits of increase or decrease, as you understand them? If not, it's back to prioritizing until this is achieved.

Now you are ready for the next step: development of the budget presentation (as outlined in chapters 7 and 8). Much of your information is at hand, due to the budget planning processes you have already accomplished. Your main objective is to put that material together in an effective presentation package. Consider the people to whom you will present the package. What do *they* think about the library? How may *they* respond to your ideas? How can you relate your ideas to *their* community or school priorities?

Have your staff critique the elements of the presentation. Rewrite, redesign, and improve what you plan to present, and *then* present. You can be confident that you are ready and can respond appropriately with specific answers and information to the questions that will be raised.

You hope you will receive approval of the budget as presented; often, however, changes must be made as a result of the presentation and review. If these changes would necessitate a major overhaul of a portion of the budget, use the information you have developed to describe to the decision makers the impact such changes will make on the ability of the library to fulfill its purposes. Then make sure all parties agree on the budget and what it will provide for the subsequent year. You may expect a formal communication from the parent organization shortly, with a copy of your approved budget.

You are now ready to implement the budget with the beginning of the fiscal year, and to manage it effectively. Chapter 10 deals with this process.

PRACTICE EXPERIENCES

1. Reproduce figure 24 from memory.

2. Discuss why it takes almost a full year to develop an effective library budget.

3. List at least four reasons why "chance remarks" are important in integrating planning information into your budget.

4. Develop and write, for your own use, the issues you consider in prioritizing programs in your library.

5. Discuss the importance of the "cut line" in budgeting.

6. List at least five ways in which the budget cycle concept assists the librarian in being an effective manager.

10
Managing the Budget

Managing the Management Tool

Once prepared and approved, your budget will become a management tool which will minimize expenditure decisions during the year. Although it helps you manage your program, *you* have to manage it; you have to expend your appropriation in a controlled, legal, and accountable way.

It is politically wise to spend all appropriated money. To underspend suggests miscalculations in your projections and implies that your requested budget was high, so that future budget requests may be disregarded. To overspend is not only bad management, but illegal. You have a legal obligation to spend appropriated money the way you said you would during budget hearings. This means that if your funding board has approved a capital outlay or expenditure for carpeting, you cannot change your mind and use that money to purchase drapes. Similarly, you usually cannot move money from one account to another without permission from the funding board.

This chapter will deal in depth with the purchasing of materials and supplies and the management of petty cash; other items are more routine and will not require as much of your time and energies. For instance, your payroll responsibilities will be discharged by verifying time worked by each employee through a payroll or timesheet. You need at least a daily accounting sheet for logging the working hours of all employees (something like figure 28). On the other hand, the personnel codes of the parent organization identify absences as they occur, and indicate payment or nonpayment (figure 29). You can complete such timesheets accurately and simply.

Without a timekeeping system, it is almost impossible to be certain of what has happened in the period covered by the payroll. Don't

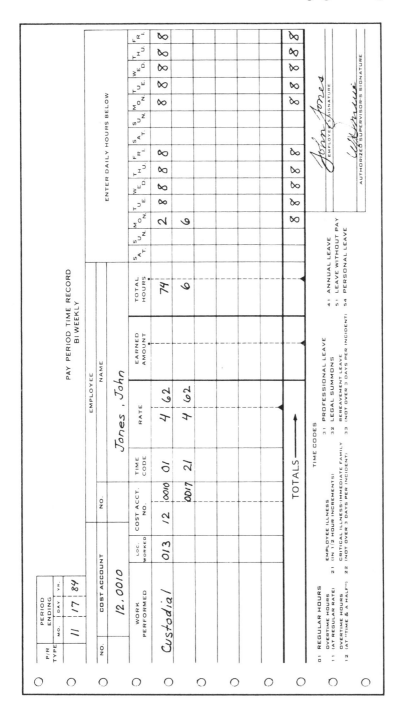

Figure 28. Pay Period Time Record (Biweekly)

Page _____ of _____

Person Absent			Hours Absent	Substitute		Periods	Comments
Last Name	First Name	Code		Last Name	First Name		

Figure 29. Daily Staff Absence Report

Absence Codes

21	Employee Illness	34	Paid Absence, Other
31	Professional	41	Annual
32	Legal Summons	51	Leave without Pay
33	Bereavement	54	Personal

trust yourself to remember these kinds of details, even if you have only a small staff for whom you are responsible. Memory is not sufficient, and examination of your records will be part of almost any audit. Figure 28 is a completed timesheet for a typical employee for a two-week period. While the interval may vary from one week to one month, biweekly is typical. Explanations on the sheet explain entries. Your organization may have other requirements; so you should have your payroll office explain them in detail until you are comfortable with the system in use.

Paying rent, paying leases, and such routine contractual obligations which fall within your budget are usually taken care of through the parent organization's accounting office. Therefore, once you have approved them and sent the approval documents to accounting, you may not be involved in the actual payments. If you are, usually you will be asked to prepare a purchase requisition to cover each billing or payment period. This process (discussed later in this chapter) is identical for all such actions, except for the cost account code and the description of the authorized purchase.

Utilities are usually handled through the accounting office as well. If they are not, the purchase requisition process is followed, using the appropriate fund account.

Fund Accounts

Most budgets are divided into classes or groups of fund accounts, such as Personnel, Operating Expenses, Employee Benefits, Purchased Services, Lease-Purchase Equipment, Capital Outlay, and Materials (see chapter 3). Usually, a fund account number is assigned by the central accounting department for each line item on the budget. For example, the Personnel account number might be 100 and each breakdown within (librarians, aides, clerical, custodial) might be 110, 120, 130, and 140 respectively. Operating Expenses might be 200; Benefits, 300; Purchased Services, 400; Lease-Purchase Equipment, 500; Capital Outlay, 600; and Materials, 700.

In many localities you may be allowed to spend money originally intended for clerical support (130) on aides (120) because you are using money intended for personnel for that purpose. You may not be allowed to move money from the 700s, which support materials, into operating expenses. In other words, you may not use money intended to buy books to pay your skyrocketing heating bills.

There are situations in which such restrictions are more or less stringent. Talk with your institution's accountant to learn the rules that govern you. Your flexibility will depend on his or her answer.

Purchasing Materials

Although you purchase materials and services throughout the year, you begin by making a request to expend—otherwise known as a *purchase requisition (PR)*. If you are the control agent, you have to verify the propriety of the purchase and the availability of funds. Usually, the PR is forwarded to the accounting department for recording in the fund account. This provides a double check on the availability of funds and it provides input into the reports you receive from the accounting department. An order is then placed with the vendor or supplier, usually by the purchasing department, in the form of a *purchase order (PO)*. With increasing frequency, these two forms are combined into a *requisition purchase order (RPO)*.

When the goods are delivered or the services rendered, someone verifies the delivery or completion of the service by initialing or signing the invoice. This certifies that payment can be made. In other words, this vouches for the delivery of goods or services. The purchase order and invoice are then gathered together to form a document which testifies to and documents the entire transaction. The document, usually called a *voucher*, is forwarded to the central accounting office, where the check is written, and this office mails it to the vendor.

Purchase Records

If you receive monthly accounting reports, you may not have to keep records of expenditures. If reports are less frequent or unavailable, you will need to set up a *ledger*. A three-ring binder, which allows easy insertion or deletion of pages, is ideal. It should be arranged by account numbers, with one page per account, and it might look like figure 30. (This example is for account number 710, from which books are purchased. At the beginning of the fiscal year, it had a balance of $50,000, which reflects the budgeted amount.)

Date of Entry 1982	Name of Vendor	Date of Invoice	Invoice No.	Amount	Balance
July 1					$50,000
August 4	Josten's	7/ 5/82		$ 500	49,500
4	Doubleday	7/14/82		250	49,250
5	Prentice-Hall	7/15/82		1,400	47,850

Figure 30. Ledger Entries

An account need do no more than accumulate the increases and decreases during the fiscal year for each budget item. By keeping records within the library, you can be "on top" of your budget at all times.

Internal Records

Even if you receive frequent accounting reports, you will keep internal records to help you make decisions about spending. Two such reports are *book encumbrances* and *released funds* caused by turnover of personnel.

Buying books, serials, and audiovisual materials presents problems not found with other purchases. When an order is placed, you do not know what discount (if any) you will receive; sometimes you do not know the list price of the item, or the shipping charge; and you cannot be sure that every title you order will be forthcoming (the book may have been advertised but not yet published; the publisher or jobber may be out of stock; or the item may be out of print).

Since most governmental accounting systems do not carry unexpended funds into the next fiscal year, you have to keep track of ordered, received, and paid-for purchases during the current fiscal year. This presents serious problems near the end of each fiscal year, when you try to spend a specific amount of money on materials whose arrival you cannot predict. To lighten the problem, you can

> Overencumber your appropriated amount by a specified time near the end of the fiscal year, such as April 1.
> Ask your jobber to send you undated invoices for materials received in the month of June.

With help from your vendor, you can date an invoice to suit your budgetary needs: either pay for it in the current fiscal year or, if you are overexpended, date the invoice "July" and pay for it out of next year's appropriations.

Encumbrances

To carry this off, you have to keep track of your encumbrances. Remember, encumbrances are formal commitments to expenditures. For instance, when you sign a purchase order but have not received the item, the money you have committed to that purchase is *encumbered*. If your parent organization is on a cash accounting system, your encumbrances must be cleared before the end of the budget year. That is, ordered items must be received and paid for before the year is over. Normally, items encumbered but not received must be canceled, rather than carried over into the next year. However, if your parent organization is on an accrual accounting system, encumbrances may be carried over to the next year.

Your fiscal account records are nearly always kept in the accounting department of the parent organization, since that is where transactions are carried out (final authorizations or checks written). However, to be aware of the status of your accounts, you may want to prepare a ledger sheet like figure 31. "Date" refers to date of entry into the ledger. "Doc." (document) and "Doc. #" (document number) identify the authorization form for ordering. When the document is a voucher, it refers back to the purchase order; and when the document is a purchase order, it refers back to the purchase requisition.

On July 1, four purchase orders were placed which encumbered $100, $50, $30, and $200. A running total of the encumbrances is kept in the Encumbered-Year-to-Date column and the same amounts are subtracted from the beginning balance, so that you always know the amount you have to work with.

Sometime between July 1 and July 6, three shipments of materials arrived, were verified, invoices were signed, and vouchers were prepared. Voucher 101 refers back to PO 1. Of the original $100 order, $50 worth of materials arrived and were paid for. Therefore, you need to add $50 to the Expended column and subtract $50 from

Date	Doc.	Doc. #	Vou. #	PO#	Expd.	Expd. Year to Date	Encum.	Encum. Year to Date	Present Balance
									$1,000.00
7/1	PO	1		1			$100.00	$100.00	900.00
7/1	PO	2		2			50.00	150.00	850.00
7/1	PO	3		3			30.00	180.00	820.00
7/1	PO	4		4			200.00	380.00	620.00
7/6	Vou	101	101	1	$ 50.00	$ 50.00	(50.00)	330.00	620.00
7/6	Vou	102	102	2	50.00	100.00	(50.00)	280.00	620.00
7/6	Vou	103	103	4	190.00	290.00	(200.00)	80.00	630.00

Figure 31. Ledger Sheet with Encumbrances

both the Encumbered column and the running total of encumbrances. Because the $50 had already been taken from the Present Balance on July 1, that column does not change.

Voucher 102 refers back to PO 2, a $50 order. The entire order was received and $50 were paid and noted in the Expended column. The Expended-Year-to-Date column is increased by $50, and both the Encumbered and the Encumbered-Year-to-Date columns are decreased by $50. The Present Balance remains the same.

Voucher 103 refers back to PO 4, an order for $200 worth of materials. In this case, the order was complete but there was a 5 percent discount, and the cost, $190, is noted in the Expended column and added to the Expended-Year-to-Date column. The original encumbrance, $200, is subtracted from the Encumbered-Year-to-Date column. Since you recovered $10 on the order, you add $10 to the Present Balance. You now have $630, rather than $620, to spend. To continue the ledger, see the following possibilities (figure 32).

On July 7 and 8, two more purchase orders were placed, for $130 worth of materials. As of July 8, you encumbered $210 and have a balance of $500 to spend.

On July 9, voucher 103.5, which refers back to PO 1, is paid. One of the ordered books is out of print; so the remainder of the order has been filled at a cost of $40—$10 less than anticipated. The Expended-Year-to-Date column is increased by $40; the encumbrance of $50 is subtracted from both the Encumbered and Encumbered-Year-to-Date columns. Because you have recovered $10, you add it to the Present Balance.

The next unusual occurrence is the payment of voucher 104. If you refer back to PO 6, you see that $100 had been encumbered, but a price increase brought the actual expenditure to $110, which is added to the Expended-Year-to-Date running total. Since you had encumbered $100, you subtract that amount from the Encumbered column, but you add the full $110 to the Encumbered-Year-to-Date column. Since you spent $10 more than planned, you subtract $10 from the Present Balance.

No significant action occurs again until November 5, when a credit memo arrives and refers to PO 8. You are receiving a credit for $40; therefore you subtract $40 from both the Expended and the Expended-Year-to-Date columns. This adds nothing to either of the encumbrance columns, and it brings your present balance to $40. It allows you to issue PO 13, which is accomplished through Voucher 114 on December 5, and your Expended-Year-to-Date column is brought to $1,000, your beginning balance as of July 1.

Date	Doc.	Doc. #	Vou. #	PO#	Expd.	Expd. Year to Date	Encum.	Encum. Year to Date	Present Balance
7/7	PO	5		5			$30.00	$110.00	$600.00
7/8	PO	6		6			100.00	210.00	500.00
7/9	Vou	103.5	103.5	1	$ 40.00	$330.00	(50.00)	160.00	510.00
7/9	PO	7		7			60.00	220.00	450.00
7/9	Vou	104	104	6	110.00	440.00	(100.00)	120.00	440.00
7/10	Vou	105	105	3	30.00	470.00	(30.00)	90.00	440.00
8/1	PO	8		8			300.00	390.00	140.00
8/1	PO	9		9			20.00	410.00	120.00
8/19	Vou	106	106	8	200.00	670.00	(200.00)	210.00	120.00
8/21	Vou	107	107	7	50.00	720.00	(60.00)	150.00	130.00
8/29	Vou	108	108	8	120.00	840.00	(100.00)	50.00	110.00
9/4	PO	10		10			60.00	110.00	50.00
9/6	PO	11		11			50.00	160.00	–0–
9/15	Vou	109	109	5	35.00	875.00	(30.00)	130.00	(5.00)
9/31	Vou	110	110	10	40.00	915.00	(60.00)	70.00	15.00
10/5	Vou	111	111	11	45.00	960.00	(50.00)	20.00	20.00
10/7	Vou	112	112	9	20.00	980.00	(20.00)	–0–	20.00
10/21	PO	12		12			20.00	20.00	–0–
11/3	Vou	113	113	12	20.00	1,000.00	(20.00)	–0–	–0–
11/5	CrM	10361		8	(40.00)	960.00	–0–	–0–	40.00
11/17	PO	13		13			40.00	40.00	–0–
12/5	Vou	114	114	13	40.00	1,000.00	(40.00)	–0–	–0–

Figure 32. Keeping Track of Encumbrances

You usually receive monthly accounting sheets which provide the breakdown of the various fund accounts and actions during that month. Normally, this is the formal organizational version of the encumbrance journal which you have been keeping. (It will therefore look somewhat familiar.) An example of such a report is presented in figure 33.

Your major function is to verify that the various expenditures and encumbrances were authorized and that books, materials, and services have actually been rendered or received, before payment is made. If a payment has been made for something you have not received, it is an error and should be speedily reported as such to the accounting office. If, on the other hand, an item has been received and payment has not been made within 30 to 90 days, you can assist your parent organization by calling it to the attention of the accounting office. One of your functions is to work with suppliers and keep their good will by seeing that they are paid as soon as possible after their goods or services have been provided. In effect, you've learned to interpret these reports by maintaining your *own* encumbrance journal.

Some accounting reports may provide analyses, such as percent of expenditures and/or encumbrances. Generally, they should match or parallel the amounts for the completed budget year. For instance, at the close of the first quarter, about one-fourth of the personnel, contract services, and utilities items should have been expended. Utilities might be a smaller percentage if the cooling system is less costly to operate than the heating system, but in general each item can readily be indexed against the amount for the past year. This is a quick check and should be made routinely for each account for which you are responsible. It makes it possible for you to identify accounts which are ahead of or behind your expectations on expenditures. If you are overexpended, you must devise a method of slowing expenditures for the next period, or risk being overexpended at the end of the budget year. If you are underexpended, you can increase expenditures, if there is need for the items in that budget category.

Other accounts (supplies, materials, and equipment) may be expended unevenly during the year. For instance, you may need to stock up on or purchase large amounts of items early in the year, or take advantage of price reductions for bulk purchases. This would place an additional burden on the supply line item early in the budget year, but will be balanced through small expenditures later. Equipment may be ordered early to provide time for vendors to process the orders and deliver the equipment by midyear. This would give the equipment account a large encumbrance, followed by a long period of inaction (during which the vendors order and receive that equipment), and then a large expenditure when the equipment is received and payment authorized.

As in all situations, practices differ. You must become well versed in the accounting procedures of your parent organization. The best way is to go to the accounting office and request training in these details early in your career. When there are questions or issues you do not understand, ask for assistance. This enhances your stature in

```
RUN DATE    3/11/83
RPT DATE    2/28/83                           END-OF-MONTH
                                       BUDGET STATUS DETAIL REPORT
                                        IN CONTROL AGENT SEQUENCE


CONTROL AGENT   11

EXPENDITURE                    PAYEE
   ACCOUNT     DATE     LOC     CODE     TYPE            P/O        VOUCHER

  85-9451    2/08/83    925    100035     VOU           51201       57896
  85-9451    2/08/83    925    100035     VOU           51202       57896
  85-9451    2/08/83    925    100035     VOU           51202       57896
  85-9451    2/08/83    925    100035     VOU           51202       57896
  85-9451    2/08/83    925    100035     VOU           51203       57896
  85-9451    2/08/83    925    100035     VOU           51203       57896
  85-9451    2/08/83    925    100035     VOU           51321       57896
  85-9451    2/08/83    925    100035     VOU           51346       57896
  85-9451    2/08/83    925    100035     VOU           51346       57896
  85-9451    2/08/83    925    100035     VOU           51346       57896
  85-9451    2/08/83    925    100035     VOU           51346       57896
  85-9451    2/08/83    925    100035     VOU           51346       57896
  85-9451    2/08/83    925    100035     VOU           51389       57896
  85-9451    2/18/83    925    100090     VOU           52107       58220
  85-9451    2/18/83    925    100040     VOU           52106       58221
  85-9451    2/18/83    925    100090     VOU           52106       58221
  85-9451    2/18/83    925    100090     VOU           52106       58221
  85-9451    2/18/83    925    100090     VOU           52133       58224
  85-9451    2/18/83    925    100090     VOU           52133       58224
  85-9451    2/18/83    925    100090     VOU           52133       58224
  85-9451    2/18/83    925    100040     VOU           52133       58224
  85-9451    2/18/83    925    100040     VOU           52133       58224
  85-9451    2/18/83    925    100090     VOU           52133       58224
  85-9451    2/18/83    925    100040     VOU           52133       58224
  85-9451    2/21/83    925    100090     VOU           52119       58232
  85-9451    2/23/83    925    100090     VOU           52184       58352
  85-9451    2/24/83    925    100090     VOU           52259       58372
                                        MONTHLY TRANSACTION TOTALS
                                         BUDGET STATUS TOTALS


  85-9452            NM INCENTIVE GRANT 82-83
                                        MONTHLY TRANSACTION TOTALS
                                         BUDGET STATUS TOTALS


  85-9461            NM STATE WORK STUDY
  85-9461    2/11/83    925    100005     P/R                       57991
  85-9461    2/25/83    925    100005     P/R                       58351
                                        MONTHLY TRANSACTION TOTALS
                                         BUDGET STATUS TOTALS

CONTROL AGENT   11                                TOTALS


                                        BALANCE LAST PERIOD

                                        TRANSACTION TOTALS

                                        BUDGET STATUS TOTALS
```

Expenditure Account: The cost account number
Date: The date of the initiation of the paperwork for this transaction.
Loc: The location code designating where this part of the organization is located.
Payee Code: The code, if assigned, for large user payees.
Type: The type of transaction, usually either payroll (P/R) or purchase order (P/O).
P/O: Purchase order number.

Figure 33. Monthly Printout of Expenditures

FEBRUARY	PAGE 74	TVG130

ENCUMBRANCE	EXPENDITURE	ADJUSTED BUDGET	UNENCUMBERED BALANCE
64.00	64.00-		
305.00	305.00-		
95.00	95.00-		
64.00	64.00-		
21.00	21.00-		
64.00	64.00-		
64.00	64.00-		
53.00	53.00-		
64.00	64.00-		
27.00	27.00-		
254.00	254.00-		
51.00	51.00-		
254.00	254.00-		
2,240.00-	2,240.00		
.00-	.00		
2,910.50-	2,910.50		
2,910.50-	2,910.50		
8,638.25-	8,638.25		
8,638.25-	8,638.25		
8,638.25-	8,638.25		
.00-	.00		
.00-	.00		
8,638.25-	8,638.25		
.00-	.00		
11,973.00-	11,973.00		
2,017.00-	2,017.00		
1,172.00-	1,172.00		
.00	56,396.00		
.00	328,640.00	220,300.00	108,340.00-
.00	39,689.00	72,522.00	32,833.00
.00	.00	72,522.00	32,833.00
.00	39,689.00	72,522.00	32,833.00
20,118.98	22,381.02	42,500.00	.00
	4,582.80		
	5,701.70		
10,284.50-	10,284.50		
9,834.48	32,665.52	42,500.00	.00
341,516.86	1,095,338.22	1,437,008.00	152.92
7,682,407.12	11,509,838.32	30,192,158.00	10,999,912.56
878,099.27-	1,540,425.26		
6,804,307.85	13,050,263.58	30,192,158.00	10,337,586.57

Voucher: The voucher number assigned to the transaction.
Encumbrance: The amount of money encumbered by this transaction.
Expenditure: The amount of money actually expended through this transaction.
Adjusted Budget: The amount of the budget line item.
Unencumbered Balance: The balance of the budget line item minus all encumbrances to date.

Figure 33. Continued

the eyes of management and provides you with the skills to carry out your responsibilities as library manager.

Personnel Released Funds

During a typical year, some of your staff will take leave without pay (LWOP); some will resign, leaving their positions vacant; some will work fewer hours than scheduled; some will work overtime. Vacancies will often be filled at either a lower or higher rate of pay. All of these situations affect your personnel budget; so you need to know where that budget stands. Figure 34 suggests a method for tracking use of these funds.

Use one card per position, as illustrated. On October 1 the reference librarian resigned, and since it took three months to fill the position, you recovered $1,167 each month. (Because the Recovered column is a running total, your Balance remained the same during the months the position was vacant.)

On January 1 you hire an experienced librarian and agree to pay an annual salary of $17,004. Note the name of the replacement and the new salary rate, as follows:

Pay Date	Amt. Paid	Encumbered	Recovered	Balance
1/1 Kate Smith, annual salary $17,004				

If you are pretty sure that Kate will be with you the rest of the fiscal year, calculate the difference between the monthly pay for Joan and Kate ($250) and multiply it by the number of pay periods left

Acct. #110   Budgeted $14,004

Name Joan Brown   Position Ref. Librn.   Pay Period Monthly

Budget Reference Page 1, line 1

Pay Date	Amt. Paid	Encumbered	Recovered	Balance
7/1				$14,004
7/31	$1,167	$1,167	–0–	12,837
8/31	1,167	2,334	–0–	11,670
9/31	1,167	3,501	–0–	10,503
10/31	–0–	3,501	$1,167	10,503
11/31	–0–	3,501	2,334	10,503
12/31	–0–	3,501	3,501	10,503

Figure 34. Personnel Released-Funds Record

Pay Date	Amt. Paid	Encumbered	Recovered	Balance
1/31	$1,417	($1,500)	$3,501	$9,086
2/28	1,417	(1,500)	3,501	7,669
3/31	1,417	(1,500)	3,501	6,252
4/31	–0–	(1,500)	4,918	6,252
5/31	1,417	(1,500)	4,918	4,835
6/31	1,417	(1,500)	4,918	3,418

Figure 35. Personnel Released Funds (Showing Personnel Change)

(6), to arrive at $1,500. This means you will be spending $1,500 more on this position than you had budgeted; so enter that information into the Encumbered column, as shown in figure 35.

During the month of April, Kate took LWOP; therefore $1,417 was added to the Recovered column. By the end of the fiscal year, the Balance is $3,418—which should equal the sums in the Encumbered and the Recovered columns.

Since each card is limited to the salary for one position, you need a summary of the cards for decision making. Create a worksheet, which is kept in pencil so you can erase and rewrite, and include the following information:

Name	Position	Budgeted Amount	Actual Pay	$ Gained (Lost)	Total

The worksheet will probably be most useful if the names and positions are entered in the order they appear on your budget document. This offers a double check on accuracy. Entries into the worksheet should be made from the cards at the end of every pay period. They will be dated entries, instead of a running commentary, because each line is brought up to date by erasing old information and replacing it with new. This is not as messy as it sounds, because most of your staff will experience no changes during the year.

As of 9/31, for example, information from Joan Brown's card will read as follows:

Name	Position	Budgeted Amount	Actual Pay	$ Gained (Lost)	Total
Brown, J.	Ref Librn	$14,004	$3,501		

On 1/31, Joan Brown's name will be erased and replaced with Kate Smith's, and Actual Pay will be adjusted to reflect an additional $1,417. The amount of money gained during the months the position was vacant will be entered into the $ Gained (Lost) column. The column total will reflect that amount of gain, $3,501, and the worksheet will look like this:

Name	Position	Budgeted Amount	Actual Pay	$ Gained (Lost)	Total
Smith, K.	Ref Librn	$14,004	$4,918	3,501	$3,501

At the end of April, the worksheet entry will be changed to reflect the LWOP:

Name	Position	Budgeted Amount	Actual Pay	$ Gained (Lost)	Total
Smith, K.	Ref Librn	$14,004	$7,752	4,918	$4,918

At any time, you can add up the Total column to find out how much money you have recovered or overspent. After you have kept records like these for a few years, you will be able to predict, at the beginning of each year, how much of your budget you are likely to recover. You can use this prediction to make staffing, hiring, and salary decisions throughout the year.

Petty Cash Voucher

Although most of your expenditures will be made by check, there will be occasions when you will have to use small amounts of cash, and it is for these occasions that a petty cash fund is established. You (or your accountant) will estimate the amount needed for a month, a check will be cashed for that amount, and the money should be placed in a secure petty cash box. To control disbursements from that supply of cash, you can use a form called a *petty cash voucher*, which might look like figure 36.

At the end of each day, the money in the petty cash box and all the vouchers must add up to the beginning balance. In other words, the balance with which the fund began, minus the voucher totals, must equal the cash on hand.

After a purchase with petty cash, the buyer should give you the receipt. These receipts are matched with their vouchers and all are

```
Petty Cash Voucher

                                        No. _____

                                        Date _____

Pay to _____ Amount _____

For _____

Approved by                Payment Received

_____      _____
```

Figure 36. Petty Cash Voucher

batched together according to account. They can be entered into a
petty cash book (figure 37).

Date	Explanation	Vou. #	Receipts	Payments	Ofc. Sup.	Post.	Other Items	
1982							Item	Amt.
July 1	Check #54 Cashed		50.00					
3	Stamps	1		20.00		20.00		
7	Pamphlet	2		.50			pam.	.50
9	Pens	3		4.50	4.50			
14	Pencils	4		2.75	2.75			
			50.00	27.75	7.25	20.00		.50
15	Balance		22.25					

Figure 37. Petty Cash Book

To replenish the petty cash fund, cash a check for $27.75. All
payments from petty cash will be charged to the appropriate accounts, at the time the check is drawn, to reimburse the petty cash
fund.

Equipment

Equipment orders almost always present problems, due either to un-
timely delivery or delivery of damaged goods. It is recommended
that, once your equipment budget is approved, you order such items

immediately. It is not unusual to wait six months for delivery, and if a piece arrives damaged, you need time to make a claim and receive a replacement.

If you wait until January or February to order and the goods haven't arrived before June 30, you will not have expended the appropriated amount. It will be returned to the general fund and, most likely, will not be reappropriated the following year. This leaves you in the position of receiving three microfiche cabinets during the following fiscal year, with no money to pay for them.

Replacement Schedule

If you create a replacement schedule for each piece of equipment as it is received, budgeting for replacements will be infinitely easier in the future. First, estimate the useful life of the equipment. The vendor will give you an estimated lifespan, but alter that estimate to reflect its use in your library. For example, if the vendor tells you a microfilm reader has a life of so many hours, use your data on all your equipment and furniture and convert the hourly use into years. The replacement schedule can be kept on 3-by-5 cards which identify equipment by inventory number, vendor, date of purchase, and cost. The cards should be filed by date of replacement.

You can look in that collection of cards each year, when you prepare your budget, to find items that should be replaced. If, after examining the furniture or equipment, you think its replacement can be postponed, you can change the replacement data and file the card again.

Using basic bookkeeping systems, you can control and account for your fund expenditures at any time during the fiscal year. Your goal is neither to overspend nor underspend your budget. To do this requires constant vigilance, but you will be rewarded by gaining the reputation of a good manager.

PRACTICE EXPERIENCES

1. Set up a ledger for each line item in your budget.
2. Identify five pieces of equipment and prepare a replacement schedule for them.
3. Without looking at the text, describe the documents that are used during a purchasing process.

4. Summarize the uses to which you put records of encumbrances.

5. Summarize the reasons why you want to know about personnel expenditures.

6. Describe a petty cash voucher.

SELECTED READINGS

Bennett, Paul. *Up Your Accountability*. Washington, D.C.: Taft Products, 1973.

Gambino, Anthony J., and Thomas J. Reardon. *Financial Planning and Evaluation for the Nonprofit Organization*. New York: National Association of Accountants, 1981.

Gross, Malvern J., and William Warshauer. *Financial and Accounting Guide for Nonprofit Organizations*. Rev. 3rd ed. New York: Wiley, 1983.

Powell, Ray M. *Budgetary Control Procedures for Institutions*. Notre Dame, Ind.: Univ. of Notre Dame Pr., 1980.

11
Zero Base Budgeting

Use of the planning technique known as *zero base budgeting* (ZBB) is less common now than it was during the early 1970s, an era of "sunshine" legislation, when laws appropriating government funds often required that the funded organizations justify their programs (and even their existence) at the end of each fiscal year. However, ZBB is useful in cut-back situations; so we include the following brief description.

ZBB requires that the cost of all programs, both current and new, be justified at the beginning of each budgetary cycle. The justification process demands that administrators look for "creative" ways of solving problems or delivering services—that the alternatives be costed out and then decisions are reached. It requires that the administrator look for services and activities of the library which can be offered at funding levels below the current one, at the current level, and at some prescribed amount above the current level. The resulting programs or packages are then arranged in priority order, from top to bottom, with their costs. At the point where expected or actual funds run out, programs below the line are dropped entirely.

Might ZBB Be Useful to You?

A systematic appraisal of the strengths and weaknesses of the budgeting process is the first step in deciding whether ZBB will be useful. If the existing budget is well controlled and gives you all the data you need to make decisions, you need not apply ZBB techniques. If your budget is expanding, you may not find ZBB critically important. If your organization is so small and limited in funding that cutting would eliminate the organization, you need not apply ZBB. But if you administer an organization which is funded beyond its bare-existence level, if you are in a cut-back budgetary situation, and if you do not have objective data to help you make decisions, ZBB may be able to help you.

If you decide that ZBB will be useful, you should be clear about your expectations and you should know for whom the information will be generated. The design of the process depends on its consumer.

Decision Units

The first step in implementing ZBB is to define the decision units— a program, function, organizational unit, or even a line item or appropriation item. The key consideration is that the decision unit parallel the responsibility for budgetary decision making within the organization. It should be the smallest organizational level possible, managed by someone who uses budgetary discretion.

Your organizational structure will help determine the decision units. Possible decision units in a public library (with branches) or in a school system are:

> Each library. If each library has a manager who is responsible for resource allocation, the individual libraries may be selected as decision units.
>
> Each service in each library. If the manager of each service (e.g., reference, circulation, children's services) in each library is responsible for resource allocation, each service may be selected as a decision unit.
>
> Each service shared by all libraries. If budgetary decisions about library services are made systemwide by identifiable managers at the main library, the services shared by libraries may be logical decision units.
>
> The entire library. This may make sense if the library is small and resource allocation decisions are made by the executive officer. This may be the case in a school and in a small public library (with no branches).

Besides the size of the organization, another consideration is availability of data. For example, a school librarian may have no more information about library costs than the amount allocated for materials or personnel. If this is the case, preparing decision packages on the library as a decision unit would be next to impossible. ZBB also requires quantifiable performance data. Decision units should be chosen so that each unit's impact is measureable; therefore unmeasured functions must be included in a decision unit that has a measurable impact.

Assigning Costs and Benefits

In the initial justification of the decision unit, the manager should first ask if it is necessary and whether its costs outweigh its benefits. To answer this question honestly, he or she must assign costs and benefits to all of the library's activities or operations. (For example, a circulation decision unit in a public library may cost $25,750, and figure 38 is a hypothetical breakdown.)

After the costs have been determined, benefits must be addressed—and this is where workload or performance measures are necessary. Performance measures for the sample circulation decision unit may be

Number of circulations per week
Number of books returned each week
Number of books to be reshelved from desks and tabletops
Number of newly cataloged titles to be shelved each week
Lag between the return of a book and its return to shelf
Accuracy in shelving
Number of interlibrary loans requested
Number of interlibrary loan requests filled

Shelving	$4,000	.5 FTE
Checking out and receiving books	8,000	1.0 FTE
	750	supplies
Overdue notices	1,000	.125 FTE
	330	postage
	150	envelopes
Interlibrary loan	3,000	.375 FTE
	470	postage
	50	copying
Reserve		
Reserve service, in-house	3,000	.375 FTE
Reserve service, delivery	3,000	.375 FTE
	2,000	postage
TOTAL	$25,750	2.75 FTE

Figure 38. Decision Unit for Zero Base Budgeting

Number of materials reserved and number picked up after notification
Number of requests to deliver materials by mail
Number of overdue notices
Number of responses to overdue notices
Amount of fines collected
Hours library is open per week.

Someone must decide whether the results are worth their cost. In other words, the judgment must be made that, for $4,000, x books can be shelved a week; for $2,000, $\frac{1}{2}x$ will be shelved, etc.

To return to the manager's justification of the decision unit: he or she must also ask if it can be eliminated. If so,

What would the consequences be?
How many ways can the decision unit's objectives be accomplished?
Which is the most effective way?
How can the efficiency of the decision unit's operation be improved?
What levels of services and costs are possible?

Decision Packages

After the decision unit is divided into a discrete set of services, activities, or expenditure items, they "translate" into decision packages. There is no single, right way of presenting decision packages. The form or format is designed to meet the needs of the organization and the expectations of the administrator. They might require such information as:

Purpose
    How accomplished
    Alternatives
    Impact (both positive and negative)
    Accomplishments/workload measures

    or

Statement of purposes
    Description of actions
    Achievements from actions
    Consequences of not approving actions
    Quantitative package measure

or

Benefits
Receivers of benefits
Consequences of not approving package
Consequences of approving 1/3 of package
Consequences of approving 2/3 of package
Alternatives

No matter how they are worded, the same questions are posed by each form.

The first package to be put together is the base package, which addresses the most important activities performed by the decision unit. This is viewed as the minimum funding level, below which the decision unit could not exist.

In the circulation decision unit, the head of circulation might see checking out, returning, and shelving materials as the minimum service level. This represents, according to our figures, $12,750 and 1.5 FTE staff. On a form, he or she is asked to outline:

The benefits of the package
Who receives them
The consequences of not funding the package
Alternative ways of providing the service
The positive and negative impacts of each

An alternative way of shelving books may be to hire high school students as pages, rather than pay a half-time employee. The advantage would be the low hourly rate. Disadvantages may be the staff time spent hiring, supervising, and training a high-turnover employee pool.

The second decision package (and succeeding packages) addresses only the increase from the previous package. In this case, the second package includes the next highest priority item, which might be interlibrary loan. This represents an additional $3,520 and .375 FTE staff. The total is now up to $16,270 and 1.875 FTE.

The third decision package may be reserve service, which will raise the cost an additional $3,000 and .375 FTE. The total is now $19,270 and 2.25 FTE.

A fourth decision package might be delivery service, amounting to an additional $5,000 and .375 FTE.

The fifth package, overdue notices, amounts to $1,480 and .125 FTE. This brings the funding and staffing to its current level: $25,750 with 2.75 FTE staff.

The current funding level is the same as last year's. It does not take inflation or increased salaries into account; therefore it directs itself to the current-dollar level, not the current level of service. If required, a sixth package might be prepared which would reflect the predicted cost of the current service level.

The Decision

Usually, no fewer than three decision packages are prepared, and seldom more than ten. The same questions about costs and consequences are asked (in narrative form) for each decision package. The head of circulation orders the packages according to his or her priority (see figure 39).

These packages are then sent to you, the director, who receives decision packages from each decision unit of the library. These packages provide a great deal of information on which to base your ranking. In this example, you may recognize that depriving the city of revenue from fines for overdue materials would be politically unwise. You therefore choose to change the order, put package 4 last (figure 40), and recompute the cumulative costs.

If you need to recover 20 percent of the decision unit's budget, you may rank the package according to a funding cutoff line.

ZBB is not only a tool to justify budget requests; it is also a resource allocation tool. If, after appropriations have been made to the library, the union negotiates salaries which cannot be supported by the appropriation, previously prepared decision packages can help you (or another administrator) pinpoint the service which can be discontinued to provide the needed money.

Priority Order	Circulation Activity	Cost	Staff	Cumulative Cost	Cumulative Staff
1	Circulation and shelving	$12,750	1.5	$12,750	1.5
2	Interlibrary loan	3,520	.375	16,270	1.875
3	Reserve	3,000	.375	19,270	2.25
4	Delivery service	5,000	.375	24,270	2.625
5	Overdue notices	1,480	.125	25,750	2.75

Figure 39. Decision Unit with Ranked Decision Packages

Priority Order	Cumulative Cost	Outcome
1	$12,750 plus	fundable
2	16,270	fundable
3	19,270	fundable
5	20,750	funding line
4	25,750	not fundable

Figure 40. The Cut Line

Subsequent Years

Will the ZBB approach be as useful to you in subsequent years as during the first year? Clearly, once the decision units and decision packages are defined, they need not change, unless circumstances change. In addition, the base need not be justified year after year. ZBB, as a management tool, can be adjusted to the needs of the moment.

PRACTICE EXPERIENCES

1. From the various ways that decision units can be identified, choose the most effective way to delineate decision units in your library and set them on paper.

2. Choose one of the decision units just identified, cost it out, and prepare decision packages—one at 80 percent of the current funding level, one at the current funding level, and the third at 110 percent of the current level. Use the form provided and fill it out completely for this exercise.

3. If you are not in a library situation, use the form provided and prepare a hypothetical justification for each of the five decision packages in the example in the text.

4. Without looking at the text, write a description of the ZBB process.

5. Note its five advantages as a management tool.

6. Justify its usefulness in your library situation.

SELECTED READINGS

Cheek, Logan. *Zero Base Budgeting Comes of Age*. New York: AMACOM, 1977.

Chen, Ching-chih. *Quantitative Measurements and Dynamic Library Service*. Phoenix: Oryx Pr., 1980.

———. *Zero Base Budgeting in Library Management: A Manual for Librarians*. Phoenix: Oryx Pr., 1980.

Appendix
Planning Charts and Networks

One of the significant elements in communicating with people in organizations is the ability to present ideas in a form other than words. There are many approaches to such a process, but in many organizational settings, due to the kinds of materials which are presented, these approaches often take the form of charts and graphs. There are a number of sources from which such skills can be learned, some of which are listed at the close of this chapter. Beyond the need for charts and graphs, there are newer techniques which relate to presentations of ideas and concepts. In this appendix, these are referred to as *planning charts* and *networks*—a compilation and condensation of approaches which have been developed during the past twenty or so years. Many of these ideas are associated with complex planning systems, and are often avoided by persons with a background in planning skills that is less than sophisticated. However, the ideas are quite workable if they are used in their simpler forms and molded to fit the needs of simpler plans.

Drawing a Picture

Effective presentation of ideas or processes often involves "drawing a picture" of that idea or process for others. Graphics can supplement verbal descriptions. The value of these kinds of pictures is that, if they are accurate, they provide a visual organization of the idea or process, reinforcing the verbal description for readers or audiences.

While there are many charting systems in use, only four of them will be presented and described:

1. Time-line charts
2. Gantt charts
3. Flow charts
4. PERT charts

Our purpose is to provide applications which will be useful in such areas as organizing work flow or planning a budget development system. But before we begin, it is important to identify several items, many of which are common to any system:

Activities to be performed
Time by which completion of these activities is essential
Time it will probably take to complete each activity
Participants in getting the job done
Relationships among the activities—which must be done before another or at the same time

Time-Line Charts

Probably the earliest forerunner of network planning was the time-line chart, which identifies activities and relates them to each other on a time continuum. The time line begins when a particular process starts, and identifies each segment of work from start to finish of the activity. A simple process might be explained through this example:

Rise	Bathe	Breakfast	Dress	Go to Work	Start Work
6:00	6:10	6:25	6:55	7:10	8:00

Each segment of the activity, from rising to beginning work, is included. Of course, further components might be added if they are critical. A segmentation of "Breakfast" would be: getting food out, cooking, setting table, eating, washing dishes. Any segment can be broken down into smaller components. However, detailed segmentation should be carried out only if this is critical to the activity, and experience with a specific process can assist the chartmaker in that determination.

The following time-line chart might represent a process for development of the library budget:

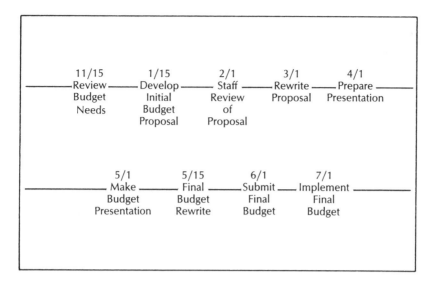

This is simple, direct, and easy to follow. However, it does not

> Identify the length of time in each segment (completion time only)
> Identify the responsibility for getting the work done
> Show interdependencies among the various segments. It assumes a linear flow of segments to complete the activity.

Gantt Charts

A further development came when Henry Gantt developed his charting system about 1900. The Gantt chart is basically a bar chart which identifies specific activities and the time periods in which they will take place. Each bar on the chart represents the beginning of the activity (where the bar starts), the length of the activity (the length of the bar), and the end of the activity (where the bar stops). Using the Getting-to-Work example, a Gantt chart would look as shown in figure A-1.

As you see, length of time can be indicated. Additionally, various activities can have overlapping time segments. For instance, while breakfast is cooking, you might be dressing. Thus the two lines would show the overlap through their length.

Figure A-2 is an example of the library budgeting process and the Gantt chart. This chart is an improvement over the time-line chart in that it

Activity	Hour				
	6:00	6:30	7:00	7:30	8:00
Rise					
Bathe					
Breakfast					
Dress					
Go to Work					
Start Work					

Figure A-1. Sample Gantt Chart

> Identifies the "time zone" in which an activity is carried out.
> Indicates the overlapping times for various activities.

However, the Gantt chart is limited in that it

> Is static. That is, interrelationships and precedent and successor relationships of the various activities are implied, not identified.
> Does not provide for "slippage" in the time it takes to accomplish a task.
> Does not identify who is involved in the activity.

Flow Charts

Another form of network planning was stimulated by data processing. Such programming is based on the need to identify (for computer operations) each step which must take place to make a program function. As the concept developed, people outside data processing adapted the flow-chart concept to other processes.

The flow chart shows the flow of tasks and the decision points in the process. Also, it has the flexibility to show recycling or looping back into the system. One of the major losses is the time factor, which is integral to Gantt and time-line charts.

Flow charts can be developed in many ways, and this chapter presents a very basic approach. A great deal of additional study is required to deal with more complex systems or to perform technical programming for a computer.

The budget development flow chart we have been using might look like figure A-3, in which boxes are used for activities and diamonds for decision points. Three advantages of flow charts are:

	Sept.	Oct.	Nov.	Dec.	Jan.	Feb.	Mar.	Apr.	May	June	July	Aug.
1. Obtain input on needs	▮											
2. Summarize needs and costs		▮	▮									
a. Summarize probable revenues		▮	▮									
b. Prioritize needs/costs		▮	▮									
3. Develop initial budget proposal		▮	▮	▮								
4. Review of proposal by staff					▮							
5. Rewrite budget proposal						▮						
6. Prepare presentation						▮	▮					
7. Make "dry run" presentation							▮					
8. Redevelop presentation								▮				
9. Present budget									▮			
10. Rewrite final budget									▮			
11. Submit final budget									▮			
12. Close out old budget										▮		
13. Implement new budget											▮	
14. Prepare subsequent year's needs											▮	▮

Figure A-2. Budget Cycle Gantt Chart

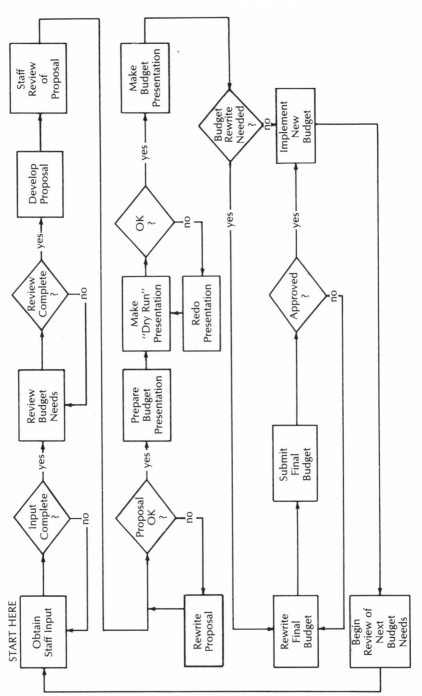

Figure A-3. Budget Flow Chart

They provide for internal recycling.
They identify decision points.
They are especially helpful with repetitive activities, since the same processes can be followed each time.

One major disadvantage of the flow chart is difficulty in representing time. Some people, therefore, include time lines which cut across the charts and act as metering devices. Also, target dates can be "built in" as part of the flow of activities. However, both devices are somewhat difficult to use satisfactorily in a flow chart.

PERT Charts

Our fourth form of planning charts and networks is the PERT system (Program Evaluation Review Technique). It was developed in the 1950s to assist planners dealing with new and highly complex activities, like planning and constructing the Polaris submarine. As other planners became acquainted with PERT, it was adapted to their needs as well. By the 1960s there were many other acronyms for PERT-type systems, such as MAPS, SCANS, TRACE, and PAR. This rapid development attests to the power of the system, as well as to its popularity.

The PERT planning system is based on identification of activities (processes) and events (accomplishments). It sets forth the various "paths" of activities and events in a network or set of lines, showing activities and events which precede and follow others. It also provides for time estimates for the accomplishment of activities. Activities on a PERT chart are shown as a line which connects two events.

A simple PERT network might look like Figure A-4. In our example of planning for the library budget, the segment 1–2 might be "review budget needs," with the event at 1 being "begin budget cycle" and, at 2, "finish review of budget needs." Events are specific points in time; they do not use money or resources, and might be thought of as accomplishments. Activities, on the other hand, are processes which *do* use resources: money, people, time. Ideally, for every activity there is an event which precedes it (*predecessor* event) and an event which follows it (*successor* event).

To begin a PERT system, we identify all the events and activities which must occur to complete an entire project or process. Some PERT charts use ovals at event points and a word or two which identify the events; others use a circle (with the number of the event) and a reference sheet (which tells what those events are). Activities

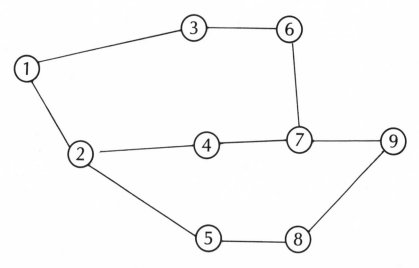

Figure A-4. PERT Chart

are similarly identified, on a separate reference sheet. The activity
line also identifies three time units in which the activity might take
place: the least possible time, the probable time, and the worst possible time.

Through these processes, a chart evolves which can display the
interrelationships among activities and which provides flexibility in
the use of time factors. As a PERT chart, our example might look
like figure A-5.

Activity on Node PERT Chart

Another form of PERT chart, rather than show the activity on the
line between two events, identifies "activities on a node," with lines
that only indicate the precedent and successor relationships. On this
type of PERT, a box is placed at each interconnecting point on the
network and the activity is described on that "node," within the box.
The value of this type of chart is that it is easier to construct without
computer assistance, and the node points contain nearly all needed
information about the activity. This avoids having supplementary lists
which define the events and activities.

Construction of the "activity on the node" chart is a matter of
listing one activity on each node card, then arranging these cards on
a large sheet of butcher paper attached to the wall: the cards show

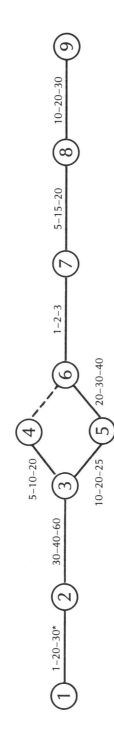

Activities

1–2 Review Budget Needs
2–3 Develop Initial Budget Proposal
3–4 Staff Review of Budget Proposal
4–6 Dummy Activity
3–5 Rewrite Proposal
5–6 Prepare Budget Presentation
6–7 Make Budget Presentation
7–8 Submit Final Budget
8–9 Implement New Budget

*Units in days.

Figure A-5. Budget Cycle PERT Chart

the precedent and successor relationships. Lines can then be drawn from card to card to show the flow. The question is always which activities come before or after others. Changes in location of a card, addition or deletion of activity cards, and the construction of the lines of flow are quickly accomplished through this approach.

A node card for budget construction might look like figure A-6 or A-7. In this case, the card becomes a planning device for which a further elaboration of the particular activity must be developed. It

Activity:	
People Involved:	
Preceding Activity:	Dates:
	Begin:
Subsequent Activity:	End:

Figure A-6. PERT Node Card (1)

Activity #		Initiator:	
Description:		Participants:	
Duration:		Cost:	
Projected:	Actual:	Projected:	Actual:
Scheduled Starting Date:		Scheduled Finishing Date:	
Actual Starting Date:		Actual Finishing Date:	

Figure A-7. PERT Node Card (2)

represents that complete activity in the chain of activities, as the line 1–2 does on the PERT chart. More or less information could be placed on the node card, as needed or desired, as long as it doesn't become too bulky.

Standard 3-by-5 cards can be used, and a rubber stamp to imprint the card design and information to be completed on each node card. A major disadvantage of the node PERT chart is that it is difficult to reduce to manuscript size.

The value of using any type of planning chart or network is that it forces you to put plans into a formal structure. This often assists in ordering your thinking and in discovering "holes" in your planning processes that might otherwise go unnoticed. Such charts are also powerful tools for communicating with your staff, as well as with your supervisors/managers.

Glossary

Activity center.   In program budgeting, a focus of organizational activities which can be separately defined.

Approved budget.   The authorized expenditure, in budget categories, approved by the parent organization before the beginning of the budget year.

Base package.   In zero base budgeting, the first-level package which addresses the most important activities performed by a decision unit.

Block grant.   Money given with no line-item restrictions.

Capital outlay.   Budget category for long-term expenditures, often over several years. Always includes costs for building construction or remodeling; often includes equipment. *Cf.* Operating expenses.

Categorical funds.   Funds granted for expenditures for specific purposes. For instance, if a private citizen or community group were to establish a fund for special book purchases, the money would be placed in this category and expended only as the citizen or group instructed. Federal or state grants which are made for special purposes would be handled similarly.

Decision packages.   Discrete sets of services, activities, or expenditure items in a decision unit.

Decision unit.   A program, function, organizational unit, or line item which is to be justified in zero base budgeting.

Encumbrance.   A claim made on a budget, before payment, for service rendered or item ordered.

Flow chart.   Visual display that shows process, movement, and distribution.

Formal organization.   The organization as it appears on a formal organization chart.

Formative evaluation.   Assessment of the processes used during a project or program. *Cf.* Summative evaluation.

FTE.   Full-time equivalent of staff. Figured by dividing number of hours worked by number of hours in the normal work week.

Gantt chart.   A bar chart, showing the times for activities in a sequence.

Guidelines.   Rule-of-thumb percentage limit on budget increases or decreases to be applied in the preparation of next year's budget. The guidelines are set by the parent organization.

Hard match.   Money given contingent on the recipient's guarantee to provide, in actual dollars, a certain amount of the funding of a project.

Increment.   Percentage to be applied to current budget to determine the subsequent budget.

Indirect cost.   Proportion of a grant request for funds to be expended by an agency in administering a grant. Usually a fixed percentage of the grant amount, established by the parent organization. Also called *overhead*.

Informal organization.   The organization as it functions.

Ledger.   A book in which accounts are kept.

Line-item budget.   The most common budget format, arranged with each category of expenditure identified on a separate line.

Network planning.   A process of indicating the relationships among the activities in a planning sequence.

Node.   A junction point, containing information, in a network chart.

Operating expenses.   Costs of operating the library, such as salaries, rent, heat, and utilities. Budgeted and expended on an annual basis. *Cf.* Capital outlay.

PERT.   Program Evaluation Review Technique—a network system of charting.

Petty cash.   Cash on hand to make small purchases.

Precedent relationship.   Identification of activities that come before others in a network chart.

Price/cost indexing.   Constructing a scale to relate (index) increases in prices or costs to a previous "base" price or cost.

Program.   Group of closely related activities formed by an activity center, around which organizational objectives can be clustered.

Program budget.   Budget constructed so that program costs are separately identified.

Purchase order.   Document to order goods or services.

Purchase requisition.   Document to notify a buying agent (such as a controller) that goods or services are required.

Replacement schedule.   System used to predict dates when equipment and furniture will have to be replaced.

Requisition purchase order.   Combined purchase requisition and purchase order.

Revenue.   Income or appropriations.

Soft match or in-kind contributions.   Agency receiving a grant guarantees to provide a certain portion of resources in donated services, such as volunteer time, goods, and equipment. *Cf.* Hard match.

Successor relationship.   Identification of activities which follow other activities on a network chart.

Summative evaluation.   Carried out at the end of a cycle of activities to determine accomplishment of objectives. *Cf.* Formative evaluation.

Time-line chart.   Shows how activities or a project relate to each other in a time sequence.

Voucher.   Documents authorizing payment.

Zero base budgeting.   Planning technique requiring that costs of all programs, both current and new, be justified at the beginning of each budgetary cycle.

Index

161

Margo C. Trumpeter is employee relations manager at Signetics Corporation in Albuquerque, New Mexico. She formerly served as director of the Lucius Beebe Memorial Library in Wakefield, Massachusetts. She has contributed articles to *College and Research Libraries, Library Journal, Wilson Library Bulletin,* and *Illinois Libraries.*

Richard S. Rounds is director of student services at Albuquerque Technical Vocational Institute. With Margo Trumpeter, he is co-author of *Budgeting for Public Libraries.*